# TOTAL DELIVERANCE
The Believer's Guide
to the Process of Deliverance

## BISHOP BOB TACKY

# TOTAL DELIVERANCE

## THE BELIEVERS GUIDE TO THE PROCESS OF DELIVERANCE

BISHOP
**BOB TACKY**

Belleville, Ontario, Canada

## TOTAL DELIVERANCE
Copyright © 2016, Bishop Bob Tacky

*All Rights Reserved. No part of this publication may be reproduced, stored in a retrieval system or transmitted in any form or by any means—electronic, mechanical, photocopy, recording or any other— except for brief quotations in printed reviews, without the prior permission of the author.*

All Scripture quotations, unless otherwise specified, are from *The Holy Bible, King James Version.* Copyright © 1977, 1984, Thomas Nelson Inc., Publishers.

Cataloguing data available from Library and Archives Canada

ISBN: 978-1-4600-0723-5
LSI Edition: 978-1-4600-0724-2
E-book ISBN: 978-1-4600-0725-9
(E-book available from the Kindle Store, KOBO and the iBooks Store)

*Essence Publishing* is a Christian Book Publisher dedicated to furthering the work of Christ through the written word. For more information, contact:
20 Hanna Court, Belleville, Ontario, Canada K8P 5J2
Phone: 1-800-238-6376. Fax: (613) 962-3055
Email: info@essence-publishing.com
Web site: www.essence-publishing.com

Printed in Canada
by

*Essence*
PUBLISHING

I dedicate this book to God
and to all those who are willing to
go through the process of deliverance.

# CONTENTS

Acknowledgments ............................................. 9
Introduction ...................................................... 11
Chapter 1: The Sin Nature ............................... 15
Chapter 2: Salvation ........................................ 19
Chapter 3: New Identity in Christ ................... 23
Chapter 4: Living Above Offences ................. 27
Chapter 5: The Process of Forgiveness ......... 41
Chapter 6: Set Place ........................................ 45
Chapter 7: The Process of Deliverance ......... 49
Chapter 8: Satanic Legal Rights ..................... 57
Chapter 9: Gifts Versus Deliverance .............. 67
Chapter 10: Destiny Repackaged ................... 73
Chapter 11: The Helmet of Salvation .............. 81
Chapter 12: Victorious Christian Life .............. 103
Chapter 13: Total Deliverance Prayer Points ... 119

# ACKNOWLEDGMENTS

I thank God for making it possible, through giving me the wisdom, grace, and resources, to write this composition. I humbly thank God and give all the glory to Him. I would also like to thank my family and the Impact Lives Church for their continued love and support.

This book is written for the demands of many believers in the Body of Christ who are afflicted by Satan and his demons. It is also a continuation of my two other books on the subject of deliverance: *Balanced Deliverance* and *Affliction vs. Deliverance*.

I would like to thank Immanuel Tacky for his help with the typing and final editing of this volume, and Christelle Bonsu for assisting in the typing of the manuscripts. I also thank Raquelle Forrester for her contributions to the editing and compilation process. Lastly, I thank Debbie Davis-West for her encouragement to write this book.

# INTRODUCTION

This book is written for both new believers and those who want to live a victorious Christian life. It will help the believer to go through the process of deliverance in order for him to enjoy the blessings of God. This book will challenge the child of God to take a holistic approach to receiving their total deliverance.

We are instructed by Jesus Christ to make disciples. A disciple is a student, and a student receives instructions from their teacher or master. A disciple must have a teachable spirit and must also act upon what they are taught. To be disciples of Jesus Christ, we must follow His teachings.

*Then they that gladly received his word were baptized: and the same day there were added unto them about three thousand souls. And they continued stedfastly in the apostles' doctrine and fellowship, and in breaking of bread, and in prayers* (Acts 2:41-42).

This scripture portion talks about how the disciples received Peter's teachings gladly and continued in the apostles' doctrines. The early believers were students of the word of God, and that is why they were disciples. They were taught the doctrine of Jesus. Jesus Christ's teachings and ministry were full of deliverance, setting the captives free. In fact, it is likely that as much as 80 to 90 percent of Jesus Christ's ministry was deliverance ministry.

In Luke 13:11-14, Jesus was teaching in the synagogue on the Sabbath day and He loosed a woman, a daughter of Abraham, whom Satan had bound for 18 years from the spirit of infirmity.

In Mark 1:21-27, Jesus went to the synagogue in Capernaum, and there was a man that had an unclean spirit, and he cried out saying, "Let us alone, Jesus of Nazareth." The people in the synagogue were amazed and astonished at the teachings of Jesus because He taught with authority and not as the scribes. Remember this is not the first time the man with the unclean spirit had gone to the synagogue. I believe he went there frequently for the reading of scriptures.

The synagogue is a place of teaching, and it is a picture of the church today. The church has become a place of good teaching, preaching, and exposition of the word of God while lacking the demonstration of the power of the Spirit of God. Believers are afflicted, captives oppressed and depressed like this man who had an unclean spirit in the synagogue. Believers are crying in the churches today for help, but no one can help them. Some pastors have ignored this ministry that was dear to Jesus, which was setting the captives free.

*The Spirit of the Lord is upon me, because he hath anointed me to preach the gospel to the poor; he hath sent me to heal the brokenhearted, to preach deliverance to the captives, and recovering of sight to the blind, to set at liberty them that are bruised* (Luke 4:18).

The Spirit of the Lord was upon Jesus Christ because He was anointed to set the captives free.

The deliverance process is a process of true discipleship. It delivers us from unseen enemies, hindrances, and barriers to growing and maturing in Christ to fulfill our destinies. The child of God cannot be possessed by demons but can be influenced or attacked by demons. If possession means ownership, then Satan cannot own the child of God. The believer belongs to God by creation and their new birth. After the believer is saved, they are out of bondage but can be captive to the activities of Satan and his demons, which is what makes the process of deliverance an absolute must.

There are three groups of people in the church today: the natural man, the carnal man, and the spiritual man. The natural man is the one who has not surrendered his life to Christ, and his sinful nature has not been crucified. The carnal man is the one who is born again but allows the flesh to control him. The spiritual man is the one who has yielded his life completely to the Holy Spirit and is led by Him. The world, the flesh, and demons work together. The world has created a system that appeals to the flesh, and when the believer yields to the flesh (that is the carnal man), it opens the door for demons to invade his life. That is why Romans 8:1 says that we should not yield to the flesh but walk in the Spirit. We have to be spiritual men to deny the demons access from invading our lives.

True disciples of Christ will always allow the Holy Spirit to minister deliverance to them. They will humble and yield themselves to the Holy Spirit to be delivered from any captivity in their lives. Deliverance ministry is vital to the effectiveness of the 21st-century church.

Therefore all believers and pastors should be aware of and engage in spiritual warfare.

> *The Spirit of the Lord is upon me, because he hath anointed me to preach the gospel to the poor; he hath sent me to heal the brokenhearted, to preach deliverance to the captives, and recovering of sight to the blind, to set at liberty them that are bruised (Luke 4:18).*

I urge every pastor who is reading this book to seek the face of God, to be consecrated, and to generate power to help the people committed into their trust to be free.

chapter one

# THE SIN NATURE

Everything God created was good and perfect. There was nothing wrong with or evil about God's creation.

*And the earth was without form, and void; and darkness was upon the face of the deep. And the Spirit of God moved upon the face of the waters* (Genesis 1:2).

The world God created was good and perfect, but sin entered into the world by one man's disobedience. As a result of that, death came.

*Wherefore, as by one man sin entered into the world, and death by sin; and so death passed upon all men, for that all have sinned* (Romans 5:12).

Sin is disobeying God's commandments. In Genesis 3, the first man, Adam, and his wife, Eve, disobeyed God's commandments. The Greek word for sin means to miss the mark. When you think of sin in this manner, think of it like having an arrow to hit a target, but whenever you attempt to hit the bullseye, you keep missing it. This is the situation of the fallen man. Man aspires to do the right thing, to be righteous or to reach God, but anytime he tries his best, he comes short or misses the mark.

*All have sinned, and come short of the glory of God* (Romans 3:23).

Anytime we try to know God or have a relationship with Him without the right way set for us, we will always miss it. Jesus Christ is the way, the truth, and the light. No one can have a relationship with God the Father except through Jesus Christ.

*Jesus saith unto him, I am the way, the truth, and the life: no man cometh unto the Father, but by me* (John 14:6).

Sin and death came into the world by Adam, but righteousness and life came through Jesus Christ (Romans 5:12).

Adam was created in the image of God. When he sinned, the image of God was not taken away from him but was affected. Therefore every human being was created in the image of God, but this image of God has been affected because of the initial sin of man. Man is dead spiritually without Christ. The breath of God that was breathed into the nostrils of man was God's Spirit, and man became a living soul. God's Spirit is in fact God. That is why man was created in the likeness of God. Man was created with God in him. The breath of God is the Spirit of God that was in man when he was created. In Hebrew, breath is *nishmat chayyim*, meaning Spirit, where in Greek, the Spirit of God is *pneuma*, meaning Spirit or soul.

After the sin of Adam, man now had a sin nature. The sin nature put man in bondage and curses and opened the door for Satan and his demons to afflict him. God made a promise to destroy the sin nature of man and redeem him from the hands of Satan (Genesis 3:15). By defeating Satan and his demons, Jesus Christ destroyed the sin nature of man and the image of God that was affected was restored. The promise of the seed of the woman that bruised the head of the serpent in Genesis 3:15 was fulfilled through Jesus Christ destroying the works of Satan on the cross .

> *Blotting out the handwriting of ordinances that was against us, which was contrary to us, and took it out of the way, nailing it to his cross; And having spoiled principalities and powers, he made a shew of them openly, triumphing over them in it.* (Colossians 2:14-15.)

After Jesus Christ defeated Satan on the cross, the image of God was restored to man. Man is made a little lower than angels (Psalm 2:8). In this portion of scripture, the word *angels* in the Hebrew is *Elohim*, meaning God Almighty. Therefore, man is made little lower than God Almighty and not angels. The fall or the sin of man made man lose his identity and status of being lower than God. Man became inferior but was created with the potential for glorification (Romans 8:30).

chapter two

# SALVATION

Genesis 3:15 gives us a picture of God's heart and plan for man. Even though man has failed God by sinning and disobeying Him, God yet makes a way of deliverance for man. God has a heart for deliverance, and He wants all of His children to be delivered from the kingdom of darkness. Because He loves the world that He created, He sent His only begotten Son to take the place of death because of our sins, so that we will be delivered and receive eternal life (John 3:16). Jesus Christ, the Son of God, has come so that we will have life and have it more abundantly (John 10:10).

When we go back to the beginning of creation in Genesis chapter 1, before God created man, God ensured that all man's needs were already made. God's desire for us is to be blessed and prosperous (Genesis 1:28; Psalm 35:27). God rejoices in the prosperity of His servants.

When we are prospering and living according to divine purpose, He is glorified, but when we are living contrarily against His will, He is displeased and Satan takes the glory. If we are bound, cursed, broke, poor, failed, afflicted, sick, depressed, oppressed, unsaved, unaccomplished, and underachieved, Satan takes the glory. When we are free, saved, delivered, healed, blessed, promoted, elevated, honoured, and favoured, God takes the glory.

How can one be saved?

Salvation doesn't come by works but by what Jesus Christ has done on the cross for us. By the shedding of His blood for us, He made atonement for us. The atonement He made destroyed the enmity between man and God. Therefore, if we believe in the work that was done on the cross, our sins are forgiven and we are sanctified and justified. We are justified by faith, and we have peace with God through our Lord Jesus Christ (Romans 5:1). Through Jesus Christ, we are justified, meaning "just as if we have not sinned before." The sin record that was against us is erased, according to Colossians 2:14.

> *Blotting out the handwriting of ordinances that was against us, which was contrary to us, and took it out of the way, nailing it to his cross.*

When we are justified, the sin record is completely erased and we have peace with God, which gives us access by faith to Him 24/7.

> *By whom also we have access by faith into this grace wherein we stand, and rejoice in hope of the glory of God* (Romans 5:2).

When we have faith in Christ Jesus, righteousness is downloaded in us. Righteousness is a big theme in the book of Romans. The Apostle Paul explained in Romans that we don't do the right things to become righteous and righteousness is not by works but having faith in the person of the Lord Jesus Christ. Abraham, the father of faith, believed God wholly and it was counted to him for righteousness (Romans 4:2-3). He was not righteous by works but by faith; therefore we cannot be righteous by obeying religious laws and rituals or by our good deeds and works. The righteousness of God is having a right standing with God or relationship with God. The righteousness of God dwells in us when we have faith and believe in Jesus Christ.

*For with the heart man believeth unto righteousness; and with the mouth confession is made unto salvation* (Romans 10:10).

God has made the salvation of man very simple so that we would not find an excuse to not be saved. The work of salvation is done by God through the death of His Son on the cross. We only have to believe in our hearts and we will be righteous; we must confess with our mouths and we will be saved. After we have believed and confessed Jesus Christ as our Lord, our sin nature is crucified and buried with Him in baptism. We are also raised with Him in His resurrection to live a new life (Roman 6:4).

When we are baptized, our old man, or the sin nature, is crucified with Christ Jesus in His death and burial. Therefore we should not serve sin again (Romans 6:6). Our spirit and the image of God that was dead and affected is now regenerated and alive to serve God and fulfill divine purpose (Titus 3:5).

The righteousness of the salvation of God is everlasting from generation to generation. Isaiah 51:11 reads:

*Therefore the redeemed of the Lord shall return, and come with singing unto Zion; and everlasting joy shall be upon their head: they shall obtain gladness and joy; and sorrow and mourning shall flee away.*

Salvation is a package; when a person is saved, God has restored and rearranged their life to possess and inherit every blessing that due them. Salvation includes the restoration of relationship with God, peace, deliverance, healing, health, favour, prosperity, material blessings, and wealth. Everything man needs is packaged in our salvation; therefore we must know the blessings of our salvation to enjoy what Christ has done for us. We are restored to our positions as sons of God to inherit the blessings of God. We have received the Spirit of adoption, where we cry Abba Father, and we are joint heirs with Christ Jesus (Romans 8:15-17). This means that we have the legal right to inherit the promises and blessings of God as Jesus Christ did. As children of God, we must know our identity in Christ in order to live a full and victorious Christian life.

chapter three
# NEW IDENTITY IN CHRIST

*Knowing this, that our old man is crucified with him, that the body of sin might be destroyed, that henceforth we should not serve sin* (Romans 6:6).

*Therefore we are buried with him by baptism into death: that like as Christ was raised up from the dead by the glory of the Father, even so we also should walk in newness of life* (Romans 6:4).

*Therefore if any man be in Christ, he is a new creature: old things are passed away; behold, all things are become new* (2 Corinthians 5:17).

Our new identity in Christ declares that the sinful nature is crucified and we are now living a new life in Christ—a new life dependant on Christ and not independent of Christ. We are in Christ, and Christ is in us. Ephesians talks about Christ in us and how we are in Christ *40 times;* this is echoed in our new identity in Christ. We are saints of Christ, we are the righteousness of Christ, we are joint heirs with Christ, we are children of God, and we are seated in heavenly places with Christ Jesus. The old lifestyle is passed away, and by the help of the indwelling of the Holy Spirit, we are now living a life pleasing to God. If we were thieves, murderers, prostitutes, adulterers, idol worshippers, liars, now we are not. Ephesians says that we put on a new man, which after God is created in righteousness and true holiness (Ephesians 4:24). We must be renewed in the Spirit of our minds (Ephesians 4:23).

The renewing of our minds deals with changing the pattern of our thoughts. Thought patterns have been established in our minds over the years, and we behave according to those patterns of thoughts. Our behaviours and characters are determined by our thought system. In order to live a new life in Christ, we must first deal with the old thought system (Romans 12:2).

Renewing your mind deals with the application of scriptures and not the recital of scriptures. You are to meditate upon the scriptures and act upon them. By so doing, you will begin to build a new thought system that will change your old behaviour. If you were a thief, you will now stop stealing and you will work to give to others. If you were a drug addict, you will stop taking drugs. If you have renewed your mind but you cannot stop sinful behaviour, the old man is still alive—it means that you need spiritual attention or deliverance ministration. This sinful behaviour may be demonic in nature with demonic foundations, which makes deliverance sessions crucial. These deliverance sessions can be done through your pastor or a deliverance minister appointed by your pastor to minister to you. Sometimes, you can do self-deliverance and you will be free, but there are some issues wherein you will need someone to minister to you.

Jesus said to the people at the tomb of Lazarus, after Lazarus was raised from the dead, to loose him and let him go (John 11:44). Lazarus could not loose himself, as he was wrapped with grave cloths from head to toe. He needed somebody to loose him. This is the exact picture of us when we become born again. We are wrapped with demonic behaviour and character that hinders us from living a victorious Christian life. We need somebody to loose and free us.

In Acts 8:9-24, Simon, the sorcerer, believed in the apostles and was baptized, but he still had his sorcery behaviour in him because he was not yet delivered.

chapter four
# LIVING ABOVE OFFENCES

*Then said he unto the disciples, It is impossible but that offences will come: but woe unto him, through whom they come! It were better for him that a millstone were hanged about his neck, and he cast into the sea, than that he should offend one of these little ones. Take heed to yourselves: If thy brother trespass against thee, rebuke him; and if he repent, forgive him. And if he trespass against thee seven times in a day, and seven times in a day turn again to thee, saying, I repent; thou shalt forgive him. And the apostles said unto the Lord, Increase our faith. And the Lord said, If ye had faith as a grain of mustard seed, ye might say unto this sycamine tree, Be thou plucked up by the root, and be thou planted in the sea; and it should obey you* (Luke 17:1-6).

Children of God, by His grace, we are above offences. Offences will by all means come, whether we like it or not. So in order to be above them, we have to be in the place of maturity. We believe that we are at the place of God by the help of the Holy Spirit, which helps us to do everything. Our Christian walk can never be successful without the Holy Spirit, and we thank God for the Holy Spirit that indwells us so that we can be above offences. We are not easily offended when people hurt us. Though we can't control it, people can speak to us in a way that we don't like and we can be easily offended. However, offences can hinder us from possessing our blessings and fulfilling our purpose in life.

Some people are always angry with everything around them, from themselves, to people in general, and their surrounding world. Child of God, if you cannot be above offences, you will not be able to become the person that God has created you to be. If the devil knows that you are easily offended, he will always use that against you. So as a child of God, you have to come to the place where you allow the Holy Spirit to help you to be able to deal with offences.

Being a part of this natural world, whether you like it or not, people will offend you. Your mother can offend you. Your father can offend you. Your son—even the people you love so much and whose lives you have invested in—they can offend you. They can offend you intentionally or unknowingly. So it's up to you to build yourself, so that you will not be affected by offences.

Offences can abort your dreams and visions. People easily run away from relationships because of offences, and this could easily make you run away from your blessing. It could be that God was about to bless you in your set place, but you became offended and ran away from your job. You also can run away from your godly relationships or even your church because of offences, but doing this can abort your dreams and visions.

There are two major ways that offences come through: either you offend someone or someone offends you.

Look at the scripture very carefully here in Luke 17:2,

*It were better for him that a millstone were hanged about his neck, and he cast into the sea, than that he should offend one of these little ones.*

Be careful that you don't offend any who are called the children of God, as every child of God is important to God. The Bible says that we have to be very careful that we don't offend any of our brothers and sisters. It says, "woe unto the person" that offences will come through.

You cannot stop people from offending you, but what you can control is not offending others. It's by the grace of God and help from the Holy Spirit that you'll be able to control yourself, even the words you speak. Some of us have loose tongues, and in our speaking we repeatedly offend people. At times you offend people unconsciously and you may be joking, but you can be offending someone when you are joking. We have to guide ourselves so that we do not become vessels of offence.

Alternatively, when people could offend us, we have to guide our hearts so that we do not become easily offended. Some people are so easily offended by every little thing that they cannot be in relationships with others. When you examine the causes of their offences, it could be annoyance, displeasure, and resentment. They have some wounds because of what somebody did or said and they are offended. They hold it in their heart, and by doing so, they block the blessings of God.

Many children of God are blessed, while some are not being blessed or enjoying the promises of God because of offences being carried in their hearts. Relationships are a must, and everybody has to cultivate a godly relationship. You cannot stand alone. You need people to interact with, and the same people you are interacting with will by all means offend you. Your husband will offend you. Your wife will offend you. The only place you will not experience offences is the grave. However, as long as you are dealing with human beings who have feelings, they will offend you, whether you like it or not. So in order for us to be above offences, we must understand and know the causes of offences. The Apostle Paul said that we are not ignorant of the devices of the enemy.

> *To whom ye forgive any thing, I forgive also: for if I forgave any thing, to whom I forgave it, for your sakes forgave I it in the person of Christ; Lest Satan should get an advantage of us: for we are not ignorant of his devices* (2 Corinthians 2:10-11).

If we are holding resentment, offences, and bitterness in our hearts against the people who offend us, we open the door for Satan to gain a foothold in our lives. This foothold enables Satan to

- function and operate against us,
- take from us our blessings,
- block us from our blessings, and
- hinder us from our blessings,

all because we are holding somebody in our hearts who offended us.

At times, we open the door for Satan to invade our lives, but we are not ignorant of his devices. We have knowledge, and we know how he operates. He may change his tricks, but he is the same devil. He will let somebody say an unkind word to us, but we must be above offences, as the Bible tells us that offences will come.

For example, Jesus said to the woman in Matthew 15:26-27, *"It is not meet to take the children's bread, and to cast it to dogs."* She could have been easily offended, but responded, *"yet the dogs eat of the crumbs which fall from their masters' table."* And through this, her daughter was made whole. Because she was not offended, she received her blessing. Offences will always make us miss our blessings.

Offences can come in many ways. One way is by misguided expectations. I have many people who are offended with me because they had an expectation that I didn't even know of, and this rests on their hearts. Once this misguided expectation is not met, people get offended. This being said, I am careful not to make promises to people.

Misguided expectations can occur in all areas of life. It happens in marriage, where you expect something from your spouse and you don't get it, so the offence starts. Some join churches with specific expectations, and if they aren't met, they get offended and move to another church.

The Bible says in Proverbs 13:12, *"Hope deferred maketh the heart sick: but when the desire cometh, it is a tree of life."* Today people are sick in their hearts because they are expecting something from someone. They are expecting something in the relationship that they are in, and because of unmet expectations they get offended.

We have to realize that we can't control people. People have so many things in their minds and so many things they are expecting; so many reasons they are friends with you or in a relationship with you. Unfortunately, as soon as they don't get what they want, they get offended.

Your role is to walk in the will of God, knowing that you can't meet everybody's expectations. Be yourself. People can be offended, and that is alright as it is beyond your control. All that you have to do is make sure that you're always above offences.

Mature people filled with the Spirit of God can also be offended. It's alright to be offended, but just don't stay there. People will hurt you, and you have feelings, but again, you must come out of it right away so that you can continue to receive God's blessings.

Offences can also take place because of your celebration, in cases where God promotes you or you are succeeding abundantly. Some people are jealous and envious of what God is doing in your life, and they become resentful toward you, because God is promoting you and you have done nothing to them. Instead of people you thought were your friends celebrating with you, they are upset.

Some people are happy when you are down and like it when you need their help. They'll tell you they are your friends and help you if you don't have anything. Because these friends are always supportive, you trust in them. You share your secrets and all of your heart's desires. Then in the blink of an eye when God blesses you and promotes you, you instantly become an enemy.

This is the same scenario that occurred with David and his older brother Eliab. As a young boy, David didn't understand that the anointing of God was upon him. In the presence of his brethren David was anointed, the youngest of all the brothers, and they saw it.

*And Eliab his eldest brother heard when he spake unto the men; and Eliab's anger was kindled against David, and he said, Why camest thou down hither? and with whom hast thou left those few sheep in the wilderness? I know thy pride, and the naughtiness of thine heart; for thou art come down that thou mightest see the battle* (1 Samuel 17:28).

Remember, like David's brother, your "friends" can see your future. They can see your destiny. They are offended because of your blessings! They are offended because of the anointing! They are offended because they see the hand of God upon your life!

Let's look at the parable of the prodigal son, in Luke 15:25-32. It describes the older brother who is coming from the field after finding out that his brother has returned.

*Now his elder son was in the field: and as he came and drew nigh to the house, he heard musick and dancing. And he called one of the servants, and asked what these things meant. And he said unto him, Thy brother is come; and thy father hath killed the fatted calf, because he hath received him safe and sound. And he was angry, and would not go in: therefore came his father out, and intreated him.*

*And he answering said to his father, Lo, these many years do I serve thee, neither transgressed I at any time thy commandment: and yet thou never gavest me a kid, that I might make merry with my friends: But as soon as this thy son was come, which hath devoured thy living with harlots, thou hast killed for him the fatted calf.*

*And he said unto him, Son, thou art ever with me, and all that I have is thine. It was meet that we should make merry, and be glad: for this thy brother was dead, and is alive again; and was lost, and is found* (Luke 15:25-32).

Always know that if at any point you turn away from God and you decide to return to Him, you'll be celebrated by God. If all men have rejected you, you are despised and no one celebrates you, come to God. God is the Father who restores your soul!

If somebody is being blessed and we are celebrating the life of the person, don't be offended like the older brother of the prodigal son. People can be offended by your blessing, and that is why you don't even want to tell some people what God is doing in your life. You have to know the people that you tell your successes to or celebrate with.

Even with weddings, people get offended. For some people, even though they may get an invitation to attend, they will not attend simply because they don't want to see what will take place. If they were to be asked why they did not attend; they will make a lousy excuse. The reality is that they were dealing with issues of the heart and they were offended. It is hard to fathom why people will behave that way, but that is the real reason. They are offended!

Offences will come, and we must be above offences. Offences can come through misguided expectations. Offences can also come through the celebration of others, such as in cases when God promotes people.

Don't share your dreams and visions with some people. Offences can come through people knowing your visions and your dreams. As soon as some people know about your visions or your dreams, some of them start praying wicked and unscriptural prayers against your dreams and your visions. They use their imaginations to fight against your visions and your dreams. There are wicked imaginations that we must hold captive and bring into obedience of God (2 Corinthians 10:5).

Some people have heard prophecies about you in church; prophecies such as you'll be married, you'll be blessed, you'll have your own business, or you'll prosper. Some of the witnesses to your prophecy will start calculating in their minds and will begin creating their imaginations. I think sometimes we have to have some private prophecies because at times when you receive a public prophecy, then you become an enemy to people.

The scriptures say that women started singing that Saul had killed 1,000 but David had killed 10,000. After that day, David became an enemy of Saul even though he did nothing to him. He served Saul with all his heart, protecting him, saving his life, and winning victories for him. David became Saul's enemy because Saul heard the women singing about the number of kills they each had.

When people know your visions, your destiny, and your dreams, they may use their imaginations to come against you, to fight against you, to stop the will of God. Child of God, no weapon of the enemy formed against us will prosper. Who has said the thing if the Lord has not commanded it? If God has not commanded it, it shall not come to pass (Lamentations 3:36-37)!

We therefore condemn every tongue that rises up against us in judgment.

We therefore condemn every imagination.

We pull their imaginations down and decree and declare that they will not prevail against us.

The counsel of the Lord will surely come to pass concerning your life.

The Lord says that they have gathered together, but I have not approved their gatherings, because I am not in it and they will not succeed (Isaiah 54:15).

Any arrows that they will throw against you will not prosper because the Spirit of God will raise up a standard against every weapon of the enemy that comes against you!

Do not freely share your dreams and visions of what God says He will do concerning your life. Be careful of the people that you tell your business plans to. Before you realize it, they will be trying to do the same thing that you said you were going to do. Rather, share your dreams and visions of God's plan for your life with people you trust and who the Lord has instructed you to talk to. The next time people try to abort your business plans and you find them doing it, say, "God will bring to pass all the visions and dreams that He has given to me!"

People also get offended by the mistakes of others. Some people blindly follow the offences of other people. If people who have influence over other people get offended, they make sure everybody is offended.

Satan gains a foothold in the church and destroys the church by bringing division in the church. Believers must understand that these are some of the things that hinder us from walking in the blessings of God.

You are praying. You are giving your tithe. You love the Lord, and you are doing the right thing you think you know, but something is blocking your blessing, and that thing can be the cause of an offence! Make peace with people!

The Bible says that if it is in your strength and in your power, try to make peace with all men (Romans 12:18). All men, not some. We are not saying that one must act foolish and allow people to come and abuse them continuously; however, the scripture says that we are to forgive.

Let's look at John the Baptist in Mathew 11:2-6. According to the scriptures, John the Baptist was offended because Jesus Christ didn't visit Him in prison.

> *Now when John had heard in the prison the works of Christ, he sent two of his disciples, And said unto him, Art thou he that should come, or do we look for another? Jesus answered and said unto them, Go and shew John again those things which ye do hear and see: The blind receive their sight, and the lame walk, the lepers are cleansed, and the deaf hear, the dead are raised up, and the poor have the gospel preached to them. And blessed is he, whosoever shall not be offended in me* (Matthew 11:2-6).

This scripture means that John was offended by Jesus. When John was put into prison, he sent his disciples to go and ask Jesus, "Are You the one who is to come?" Remember, John was the same person who baptized Jesus and saw the Holy Spirit come upon Him in the form of a dove. God spoke from heaven and confirmed that He was "My son, my beloved Son," which indicates that Jesus was the Messiah!

However, when John was in prison and Jesus didn't go and visit him, John was offended. Sometimes, you may be in situations when people don't come and visit you. You get offended. You're sick, and people don't come visit you. You get offended. Nobody calls you. You get offended. You are going through your trials, your temptations, your difficult times. No one calls you to encourage you. Automatically you'll be offended.

In John's case, he was offended especially because he knew that Jesus was the Messiah. So he said, "Go and ask Him, 'Are You the true Messiah?' A Messiah that when I am in prison will not come and visit me? What kind of Messiah is this? I'm in prison. You are my cousin. I baptized You, and I thought when You heard I am in prison, you would come to the prison, and maybe command the prison doors to be open and free me. You never showed up!"

You see, sometimes challenges and offences will bring some doubt about the credibility of people around you.

Is He the true Messiah? Is He the true man of God? Is He the true prophet? When you had no problems, you never doubted if Jesus was the true Messiah, but now that the problems have arisen, you start questioning things as a result of being offended.

Jesus sent a message to John about His credentials as Messiah to confirm what he already knew. Sadly, not long after this, John was killed. Offences cut off his destiny. John's situation could have changed, but he had so much offence in him.

As for us, we have to know how to deal with offences. We are not ignorant of Satan's devices (2 Corinthians 2:11).

- We don't give him a foothold in our lives.
- We don't become bitter.
- As soon as we recognize that we are bitter and offended, immediately we have to release it.

As an emotional being, if you do not release offences, the enemy will use the hurt, the pain, and the bitterness to hinder you and fight against you. So therefore, child of

God, when you are hurt, when you are offended, release the hurt, release the pain. Let it go.

The Bible says in Matthew 6:12 and Luke 11:4 that we should forgive. If people offend you, forgive them. Don't hold it against them or hold onto it forever. When you forgive people, you are acting with wisdom as opposed to ignorance. You are smart, because you are releasing them from your hook to God's hook and allowing God to deal with the person. By releasing them and forgiving them, you are letting God know that you have nothing to do with this thing; you are saying, "Father, take care of this."

By doing this, the end result is that you are separating yourself from the offence and you are doing a good thing for yourself. There is so much power in forgiveness. When you are forgiving, it doesn't mean that you forget, but you release the offence to God for Him to take action.

When the Bible says that God has forgiven us and He will not remember our sins anymore, it means that God will not bring our sins against us again and He will not remember them. As believers, we need to follow God's model and not bring any offences against other people. We are to release our bitterness and let God deal with it. That is what Jesus did for us. We sinned, and we were supposed to be punished and die, but Jesus forgave us and took our place of death. Jesus did that for us so that we could be free. That is what we believers are to do. We live with the consequences of the sins of people when we forgive and give them to God. If we do that, then we release the blessings of God.

I pray that you'll always be above offences by the help of the Spirit of God. I pray that you will guide your heart so that you will not hold onto resentment and that you will always release people immediately so that you can walk in the blessings of God. As you have received the engrafted word of God, I invite you to say this prayer so that you will be free from offences and receive the blessings of God:

> *Thank You, Jesus, for the work done on the cross. You took my place of death and punishment. You have forgiven me on the basis of the work done on the cross. I release and forgive those who have offended me in Jesus Christ's name. I declare I will not give Satan a foothold in my life. I am not ignorant of his devices. I terminate and uproot every trace of bitterness in me. I release the manifestation of any blessing due me in Jesus Christ's name. Amen.*

chapter five

# THE PROCESS OF FORGIVENESS

In a quiet place, ask God to bring to mind any person you need to forgive. Write down their name(s) and the specific reason for which you are forgiving them. Go through each name with a prayer of forgiveness for the specific offence. Thank God for releasing them from your heart.

We are delivered from the kingdom of darkness and translated into the kingdom of God's Son (Colossians 1:13). The handwriting of ordinances that was against us has been erased.

> *Blotting out the handwriting of ordinances that was against us, which was contrary to us, and took it out of the way, nailing it to his cross* (Colossians 2:14).

In the secular literature, the "handwriting" spoken of in Colossians was an I.O.U. signed by the debtor, a certificate of debt consisting of decrees. In this scripture, this decree refers to the law of Moses. Man is unable to obey the law, but by the grace of God and the blood of the eternal covenant, his sin has been paid for and erased. Therefore, Satan's attempts to bring our past sins against us cannot prevail if we stand on this scripture.

Now we are forgiven, sanctified, justified and are righteous by faith. Being a child of God does not mean that we will not be offended or hurt. Offences will by all means come, but how we deal with the offences will determine whether we live a victorious Christian life or not. The scriptures say that offences will always come but woe unto them that they come from. If we don't forgive, we give Satan a foothold to invade our lives (2 Corinthians 2:10-11).

When Jesus taught on prayer, He made sure to talk about forgiveness (Mark 11:25, Matthew 6:12). We have received forgiveness from the Father, so we should also forgive others. As a servant and minister of Jesus Christ, people who I minister to and help are the same people that hurt me. If I don't forgive people who offend me, I cannot be effective in ministry because people will not always do what I expect of them. In relationships and dealing with human beings, conflicts will always come, but if they are handled properly, we become mature. Conflicts may seem to be a negative thing, but it can be a vehicle for maturity, healthy relationships, and blessings.

Offences and conflicts will come, but when they come, we should not let Satan take advantage to destroy divine relationships and take away the glory from God. When conflicts and offences come, we should maximize the opportunity to allow blessings to come out of it so that glory will be given to God.

Over the past 29 years we have been engaged in deliverance ministry, God has used us to bring freedom into many people's lives, but some have allowed Satan to use them to hurt us. In the early years of the ministry, when these things happened, I did not understand and it didn't make sense to me. These are people who we invested our time and money in, and we risked our lives to help them and their families. I have learned not to react to these disloyal and ungrateful people. It is the enemy who influences these people so that he can take away their deliverance and gain a foothold in their lives. The devil knows that through us they have obtained their deliverance and his work is destroyed, so he tries to break the relationship they have with us.

I have noticed that the devil uses deception against these people. He deceives them by putting evil thoughts in their minds against us. When these thoughts are put in their minds, they act out by offending and hurting us. This has taught us a big lesson to not react when we see such behaviours. We have also learned not walk in the flesh but to control our emotions. Even though we have helped these people and they have hurt us and disappointed us, we understand that it is part of Satan's attacks to hinder and stop the deliverance process. We have to learn how to be sensitive to know the source of these offences and hurts.

*For if ye forgive men their trespasses, your heavenly Father will also forgive you: But if ye forgive not men their trespasses, neither will your Father forgive your trespasses* (Matthew 6:14-15).

*And their sins and iniquities will I remember no more* (Hebrews 10:17).

Forgiveness is not forgetting. Forgetting may be the result of forgiveness but not the means of forgiveness.

Forgiveness is a key to our deliverance. Forgiveness is critical to receiving our deliverance. We needed to be forgiven, and God forgave us according to His mercies. He is a merciful God and forgives us, so we must also forgive others. Whenever we forgive people, we are doing it for ourselves.

chapter six

# SET PLACE

Our set place is a place where God has ordained for us to fulfill our destiny. It is a place where we live out our passion and vision. God has a set place for every one of us to fulfill our divine purpose and destiny.

*And have made of one blood all nations of men for to dwell on all the face of the earth, and have determined the times before appointed, and the bounds of their habitation* (Acts 17:26).

God has appointed a place for us to dwell in a particular time to fulfill our purpose in life. The human body is one but has many members. All the members of the body have been put in their place for a specific function and purpose. They function properly in the set place in which they have been positioned. Therefore there is a lot of importance behind where they have been placed for the proper functioning of the whole body (1 Corinthians 12:12). God has a set place for each of us, and we must identify our set place in order to prosper and glorify God. There is a set place for us in ministry, in church, geographically, in marriage, in business, in education, and in gifts.

## HOW DO YOU FIND YOUR SET PLACE?

- The Spirit of God must bear witness with your spirit, and you must have peace in your spirit (Romans 8:16).
- You are able to live out your passion and vision.
- You bear fruits in your set place (Psalm 1:3).
- You don't struggle in your set place as you struggled in other areas.
- Your gift is manifested and you excel in your ministry at your set place.
- Challenges will come, but you will overcome them and they will make you better and matured.
- Satan and people will try to move you out of your set place.
- You are celebrated at your set place.

After you have identified your set place, you must be loyal and not allow the enemy to deceive you to move you out of your set place. The devil knows that if you remain loyal and faithful to your set place, you will prosper, so he tries to move you out of it.

There are some Christians who are always hearing voices, claiming that God is speaking to them to move out of a place that one time had been their set place. When they move from their set place, they prematurely abort their blessings and visions. Some Christians always move from place to place, church to church, ministry to ministry, claiming that they are in transition and that God always wants to do something new for them. So they use the phrase, "We have to move on." Such Christians have what we call an "orphan spirit." An orphan spirit is unstable and is always looking for acceptance in different places. They are also not loyal and faithful. Therefore, they cannot be in one place for a long time, so they move and they miss their blessings. They don't grow and bear fruits because they are not planted.

Psalm 1:3 says that those who delight in the law of the Lord and meditate upon it day and night are like a tree planted by rivers of water, which brings forth its fruits in its season. When you are planted like a tree in your set place (by the rivers of water), you will prosper and bear fruit and your leaves will not wither and whatever you do will prosper. If you are not in your set place, nothing you do will prosper. You will struggle, be confused and frustrated and you will go nowhere in life.

I pray that you identify your set place and that you remain loyal in your set place. I therefore declare that as you are planted in your set place, nothing can uproot you, nothing can abort your blessings, nothing can hinder you from prospering. You will be fruitful, you will increase and be elevated, and whatever you do will always prosper in the name of Jesus Christ.

chapter seven

# THE PROCESS OF DELIVERANCE

Deliverance is a three-stage process: we are saved, we are being saved, and we shall be saved. Man is made in three dimensions: spirit, soul, and body. When we accept Jesus Christ as our Lord and Saviour or when we become born again, it is our Spirit that is saved; our soul, which is our mind, will, and emotions, also goes through the process of deliverance. This can be done through hearing and studying of the word of God or deliverance ministrations. Finally, our bodies shall be saved when Jesus Christ comes for the second time.

> *Who delivered us from so great a death, and doth deliver: in whom we trust that he will yet deliver us* (2 Corinthians 1:10).

In this portion of scripture, you can see deliverance in three stages. First of all, he said, "who delivered us," which is past tense—our spirit saved. "And doth deliver" is present tense—our soul going through the process of deliverance. "In whom we trust that he will yet deliver us" is future tense—our bodies will be redeemed when Jesus Christ comes again for the Church.

Man has a spirit, a soul, and a body. Our spirit was dead, but by the Holy Spirit, it has been regenerated out of death and we are now alive. Our spirit knows God. We go through deliverance regularly as we cleanse and sanctify ourselves daily.

The world is contaminated with evil. As long as you are a child of God, Satan will always come against you. You are anointed and graced by God, and because of your gifts and destiny, the enemy will always come after you. You are created by God in His own image. You are born of the Spirit of God, and the enemy cannot take ownership of you. The devil cannot own you because he has not created anything. Do not be afraid of the enemy.

Some Christians seek psychics and palm readers because they need help and need to be delivered. If the church cannot help them, they will seek help elsewhere. The church is the place where the afflicted and the bound must be set free! The Spirit of the Lord has anointed us to preach good tidings to the poor and to set the captives free. They are bound, but they must be loosed and set free. People of God should not go to church and return home unchanged all the time. It is our time to be free and joyful. Where there is deliverance, there is joy.

## WHY IS DELIVERANCE A PROCESS?

God told the Israelites that He would drive out the nations from the promised land little by little.

> *And the Lord thy God will put out those nations before thee by little and little: thou mayest not consume them at once, lest the beasts of the field increase upon thee* (Deuteronomy 7:22).

The nations would not be cast out before the Israelites in the promised land at once because the beasts would consume them. In the process of deliverance, strategically and step-by-step we are free from the strongholds of demons in our lives. Sometimes deliverance can occur instantly, but in most cases we are free little by little. This is why continuous ministration is required for total deliverance. Sometimes people become Christians, and we expect them to be perfect and receive total deliverance, forgetting that they had demonic strongholds for many years of their lives before getting saved. They need to go through the process of deliverance in order to receive total freedom. As they go through the process, strongholds are loosed step by step.

Deliverance has to be a process. If we don't understand spiritual warfare and how to maintain our deliverance, we invite more demons to reside within us. We must have more of the word of God in us to keep the demons out. Exodus 23:29-30 says,

> *I will not drive them out from before thee in one year; lest the land become desolate, and the beast of the field multiply against thee. By little and little I will drive them out from before thee, until thou be increased, and inherit the land.*

There are giants in the promised land. We must be prepared and ready to deal with them. If we were to take possession of the land all at once, the giants would rise up against us and overtake us. When we possess the land step by step, we will mature and experience permanent and total deliverance. God will give us enough time to have more of His word in us in order to maintain our deliverance one step at a time.

## SIEGE WARFARE

Spiritual warfare and the deliverance process is similar to siege warfare experienced around the time of 1400 BC.

Under siege warfare, the invading army surrounded a city, blocking all access in and out. The inhabitants would be focused on maintaining themselves inside the city without starving to death or dying of thirst. In a long standoff, a siege could often last two or three years.

Siege warfare is similar to the deliverance process in that it does not take place in one day. The invading army must have a strategy that will pull down the walls of the city over a period of time. Archeologists have discovered that the typical city-state had a surrounding wall measuring about 50 feet high and 50 feet wide. You can see what a huge task it would be to destroy such a wall over a few days or weeks. I liken this to demons and their methods of establishing strongholds by invading lives and building "walls" for many years.

In the process of deliverance, the minister must ask God for a strategy for the captive's freedom. God usually provides an organized action to implement. This action takes time and it is a process. There is no drive-through deliverance, but it is a process. You must be patient to receive holistic deliverance.

Someone can ask, is God not powerful to set the child of God free instantly? I will argue that demons cannot stand the power of God.

> *God hath spoken once; twice have I heard this; that power belongeth unto God* (Psalm 62:11).

All power belongs to God, and God is more powerful than Satan and his demons. He defeated them and they couldn't stand before Him (Colossians 2:15). God allows us to be part of the process, yet sometimes we give Satan and his demons legal rights in certain areas in our lives. God or the deliverance minister cannot force anyone to relinquish the rights he has given to the enemy over his life. In some cases, known and unknown covenants and agreements have been made with the enemy and must be broken and destroyed in order for the child of God to be free.

A lack of knowledge of the child of God can also prolong the process of deliverance. If both the oppressed and the deliverance minister do not know the cause of the problem or what they are dealing with, this can prolong the process. Discernment of spirits is vital to the situation; you must know the spirits that are involved in order to cast them out. In Mark chapter 9, Jesus asked the father of the young boy who was possessed how long the son had been afflicted by the demons, and the father responded, "Since he was a child." This shows that investigation is important in the process of deliverance, because it gives us knowledge to address the issue specifically. In Mark 5:9, Jesus talked to the spirit that was in the possessed man:

*And he asked him, What is thy name? And he answered, saying, My name is Legion: for we are many* (Mark 5:9).

We should be careful not to always ask the name of a demon. Jesus had His reasons why He asked at that particular time. Knowing the name of the demon helps us to command them by their name to come out. We should be careful not to be addicted to deliverance ministrations, wanting to be prayed for at all times, constantly demanding deliverance sessions. We must be responsible for our deliverance rather than depending solely on the deliverance minister all the time.

Some people are addicted to demonic manifestations, and they love to attend the deliverance sessions. With some cases, before we start ministration, these same people have already started jumping and manifesting because they know the pattern and they end up wasting their time and that of the deliverance minister. Some people have also gone through many deliverance sessions with different deliverance ministers. They become familiar with the deliverance process, and it can become so routine for them that they do not get any results or freedom.

We should be very careful not to form a method or a formula during the deliverance process, but allow the Holy Spirit to work in the life of the person. Therefore, deliverance comes by the Holy Spirit. Jesus said, *"If I cast out devils by the Spirit of God, then the kingdom of God has come unto you"* (Matthew 12:28). In the process of deliverance, we depend solely on the Holy Spirit to bring total deliverance!

I don't believe in the manifestations of demons and people not being set free. I believe however that after the demons have manifested, they should leave and people must be set free. I believe in getting results rather than just manifestations.

Some people will argue and ask why some Christians manifest the same way during deliverance sessions if they are already free. I believe that some Christians are free in certain areas of their lives, but they may be bound or afflicted in other areas. There may be hidden or unknown demonic covenants and strongholds that need to be broken and destroyed. Some of these covenants are generational demons that are stubborn; they don't easily let go, and continuous ministration needs to take place so that they loose their holds and leave the child of God. That is why the child of God must go through the process of deliverance.

Some stubborn demons have different layers where they hide in the human body, so the deliverance minister must identify where they are hidden and torment and command them to come out. It is imperative for the deliverance minister to have knowledge about where the different demons hide in the human body. Witchcraft spirits, marine spirits, abortion spirits, suicide spirits, and immorality spirits all have their places where they hide in the human body. These spirits must be tormented by the fire of the Holy Ghost and by the blood of the eternal covenant. The demons must be exposed by the truth of God's word, which is light, and they have to be commanded out in the name of Jesus Christ.

chapter eight

# SATANIC LEGAL RIGHTS

Satan must have a legal right in order for him to invade your life, take your blessing, and afflict you. If he has no access into your life, he cannot invade you. Ephesians 4:7 says not to give place to the devil. Meaning you *can* give place to the devil. In John 14:30, Jesus said, *"the prince of this world cometh, [but he has] nothing in me."* There is nothing of Satan in Jesus that he can use as a point of contact to have access to Him, which is why Jesus said that Satan could not touch Him. If Satan has nothing in you and doesn't have the legal right, he cannot invade your life; he cannot afflict you, oppress you or steal from you.

We must block and deny Satan from having access into our lives. We must terminate and destroy all of Satan's assignments against us and cause him to back off. Even though we are blessed by God, not one of us is exempt, and we all still have some issues that we have to address in our lives.

*Many are the afflictions of the righteous: but the Lord delivereth him out of them all* (Psalm 34:19).

Even though the righteous is blessed, he still has problems in his life, and God will deliver him from all of them.

We are the seed of Abraham, we have been promised the blessings of Abraham, yet we are not experiencing them. We are not living according to what the word of God says we are. There are some things that are blocking the manifestations of our blessings, and these things have held us captive and hindered us for many years.

In John 14:30, Jesus said, *"the prince of this world cometh, [but he has] nothing in me."* So if the prince of this world, who is Satan, comes and has nothing in Jesus, Jesus is saying that Satan has no legal right to touch Him. Satan and his demons cannot touch or have access to us without the legal right. He can only touch and have access to our lives, families, or ministries if he has a legal right. There is nothing of him in us for him to have access to us. The only time he has access to us is when he has deposits in us that become a point of contact for him to afflict us. As a child of God, we are not automatically protected; the promises of God manifest when they are enforced. The promises of God will never manifest if they are not enforced, and they will only come to pass when we wage warfare. That is why 1 Timothy 1:18 says, *"This charge I commit unto thee, son Timothy, according to the prophecies which went before on thee, that thou by them mightest war a good warfare."*

We wage warfare with the promises of God to manifest; things happen because we make them happen. If we don't deal with the things that have given Satan the legal right, he will always hinder us from enjoying the blessings of God. This means that we can be a child of God living a holy life, giving our tithes, but if we don't close the doors that have given Satan legal rights, we will not see the manifestations of the promises of God in our lives. When we don't see the blessings of God manifesting in our lives, it causes us to question God. Then we come to find out that the problem is not God but rather the issues in our lives that have not been addressed and have given Satan a foothold in our lives. Sometimes we compare ourselves with others, thinking that we live a holier life than them but they are experiencing the blessings of God more than us. Everyone's battle is different; some may be dealing with heavier problems than others. Even though we love God and may be doing the right thing, we may have given Satan the legal right to invade our lives, and he has gained an advantage and afflicted us.

*And the Lord said unto Joshua, This day have I rolled away the reproach of Egypt from off you. Wherefore the name of the place is called Gilgal unto this day* (Joshua 5:9).

Why did God say that He rolled away the reproach of Egypt from Israel, who had been delivered from Egypt forty years before? They were delivered forty years before, but they were still carrying the issues of Egypt with them. This is a picture of the child of God today; we have been delivered from the kingdom of darkness, but there are issues in our lives that we have not dealt with. The children of Israel had not dealt with some of the Egyptian issues in their lives, so Egypt was still with them. Egypt had to be cast away from them before they could possess the promised land.

The children of Israel had to be circumcised (Joshua 5:7), and this was the second circumcision of the children of Israel because all of the numbered men were circumcised at the first time, and all of them died due to disobedience. A new generation arose who were not circumcised; and God could not take uncircumcised people into the promised land.

Uncircumcised people cannot possess the promised land: you must cut off some Egypt (world) out of your life. You must cast some demons out of your life before you can possess the promises of God. Jesus said when He cast out devils by the Spirit of God, then the kingdom of God comes (Matthew 12:28). Demons are hindrances to the manifestation of the kingdom of God. The kingdom of God is righteousness, peace, and joy (Romans 14:17). In order for you to experience righteousness, peace, and joy (the kingdom of God), demons must be cast out of you. The children of Israel came out of Egypt, but they had reproach. We are out of the world, but we have reproach around us. The reproach can be rolled away in your life by divine authority. The only person who can stop Satan and his activities in your life is you. The Bible says give him no place (Ephesians 4:27).

The only place that Satan can have in your life is that which you have given him. If you don't give him any place, he has no place in your life. Therefore, if you want him to be cut off your life, he can be cut off. If he has legal rights to invade your life, it's because you gave it to him.

Satan can also have legal rights in your life through your bloodline.

*Thou shewest lovingkindness unto thousands, and recompensest the iniquity of the fathers into the bosom of their children after them: the Great, the Mighty God, the Lord of hosts, is his name* (Jeremiah 32:18).

Things that we inherit from our ancestors can give Satan the legal right into our lives. The sins of our ancestors open the door for Satan to have legal rights in our lives.

In Genesis 12, God promised Abraham that he would be the father of many nations, but he had no seed at the time. The seed of this promise was fulfilled in the person of Isaac. Isaac had Jacob, and Jacob had twelve sons. The twelve sons of Jacob became the nation of Israel, and Israel went into bondage for four hundred years until they finally came out of bondage. Out of the twelve tribes, Judah was chosen for the fulfilment of the promise of the seed of Abraham to be the father of many nations. Through Judah came David, and through David came Jesus Christ, the Messiah, who came to redeem us from the kingdom of darkness. Through Him, the promise is fulfilled that anyone who believes in Him is a seed of Abraham (Galatians 3:29). The promise is fulfilled, and Abraham is the father of many nations.

When Israel came out of Egypt, they were not yet a nation. Three things make a nation: a people, a constitution, and land. When they came out, they had a people and a constitution but no land. When they possessed the promised land, they became a nation. When Israel came out of Egypt, they had a people, and a constitution in the wilderness. The constitution was the Law of Moses that governed them on how to worship, what to eat, and what to do. The constitution that was given to the Israelites was to govern their lives so that they would prosper in the land. After they became a nation, they went through the process of the sin cycle. They didn't have a king, but they had judges. In the Book of Judges, we see the children of Israel always sinning. When they sinned, they opened the door for their enemies to afflict them. When they were afflicted by their enemies, they cried unto God for deliverance and

God delivered them through a judge. They were going through the process of a sin cycle.

The Book of Judges is referred to as the book of the sin cycle because of the repeated sin and repentance of Israel. When this happened, God would raise up a judge to deliver the Israelites from their enemies and then they would repeatedly go back to their sins. That is why they had many judges like Samson, Deborah, Gideon, etc. to deliver them from their enemies.

Today, God has anointed skilful men and women to help us to be free from our enemies through Jesus Christ, who is the captain of our warfare. In the Old Testament, God commands deliverances to His children.

*Thou art my King, O God: command deliverances for Jacob* (Psalm 44:4).

In the New Testament, the believer commands deliverances to the captives because he has been given authority and power over the works of Satan.

*Then he called his twelve disciples together, and gave them power and authority over all devils, and to cure diseases* (Luke 9:1).

"By divine authority, I command deliverances and freedom to anyone that is afflicted, bound, and captive to Satan in the name of Jesus Christ."

## DESTROYING BLOODLINE ISSUES

In the Book of Genesis chapter 38, we are introduced to one of the sons of Jacob, called Judah, who engaged in incest with his daughter-in-law Tamar. Judah slept with his daughter-in-law Tamar, and because of that, a curse was placed in his life and his seed, and the issue was not dealt with. At that point in time, Israel was a nation, had a people, a constitution, and a land, but they didn't have a king and they wanted a king and not a judge, so they cried to Samuel for a king (1 Samuel 8:4-7). According to Genesis 49:10, Judah is a law keeper, law giver, will rule his people, and will give instruction and is a king; therefore the king must come from the tribe of Judah. They were requesting a king to be like the other nations, and God gave them their request. God gave them Saul, but it was not His choice (1 Samuel 10:17-25).

I believe one of the reasons why God could not give them a king at the time was because of the sin issue in the tribe of Judah that had not been dealt with. Judah was supposed to be the king, but because of the incest that occurred in his life, the curse was passed on to his seed and delayed the promise of God for four hundred years. In the book of Judges, the Israelites went through the cycle of sin without a king.

That is what happens to us when we give Satan the legal rights to our lives. He hinders or brings setback to the manifestations of the promises of God concerning our lives, ministry, and destiny. We must destroy the door that was opened through the bloodline in order to see the fulfilment of the promises of God.

After King Saul was rejected by God, He gave them His choice, King David from the tribe of Judah. David committed adultery because of the sin of lust and immorality in the bloodline of Judah that was not dealt with. Even though he was anointed king by God, he had inherited issues in his bloodline that were fighting against him (Psalm 51:5). The problem of David was not just the adultery but the murder that he caused. Many people died in battle because he wanted to cover up his sin. He sent Uriah, Bathsheba's husband, to go the hottest place of battle, where he knew he would die. He set him up; David gave him a letter that contained his death sentence.

Sometimes, the enemy will set us up and put us in places where we are not supposed to be, but I pray that we escape all the snares of our enemies. May our souls escape every trap and snare of the enemy like a bird (Psalm 124:7).

Judgment was pronounced upon David because of the sin he committed and the thousands of Israelites who died. The scripture says that the sword will not depart from his house. *"Now therefore the sword shall never depart from thine house; because thou hast despised me, and hast taken the wife of Uriah the Hittite to be thy wife"* (2 Samuel 12:10). God forgave David, and he was the man after God's heart, yet the sword would not depart from his house. He still had to reap the consequences of the murder he committed. God will forgive us, but when we give the demons the legal right in our lives, they will not forgive us.

Deuteronomy 32:2 says the bastard will not enter into the congregation of the Lord to the tenth generation. According to the genealogy of Jesus Christ in Matthew 1, David was the tenth person in line of the bloodline curse that was placed on Judah. David did not deal with the issue in the bloodline, and that is why I believe he sinned. If we don't deal with the bloodline issues, we give Satan the legal right to invade our lives.

Also because David did not deal with the sin in the bloodline, his first son, Amnon, raped his own half-sister Tamar (2 Samuel 13).

The lust in Judah was transferred to David and his sons; that is why Amnon raped his sister. David did not do anything about what Amnon did to Absalom's sister (full sister), so Absalom took revenge by killing Amnon. So we can see that the judgment that was pronounced on David was active in his house, and Satan made sure that the sword would not depart from his house. Absalom went into exile after killing his brother Amnon and returned back later. After his return, he rebelled against his father and tried to take the throne from him, and he was killed by the sword. The sword would not depart from David's house because Satan had the legal right to ensure that the judgment pronounced was active.

Through the work done on the cross, any legal right that Satan has over our lives can be destroyed and we can have permanent victory in the name of Jesus Christ. I terminate and destroy every door that has given Satan the legal right in your life by the blood of the eternal covenant. And I command any spirit hiding in your body to come out in the name of Jesus Christ.

chapter nine

# GIFTS VERSUS DELIVERANCE

Today's Christians do not believe in the process of deliverance, but they will seek the gifts of the Spirit.

*He that believeth and is baptized shall be saved; but he that believeth not shall be damned. And these signs shall follow them that believe; In my name shall they cast out devils; they shall speak with new tongues* (Mark 16:16-17).

This scripture portion says that when you believe and you are baptized, you shall be saved, and when you don't believe, you will be condemned. Note that the first sign that follows the believer is *"they shall cast out devils,"* and this echoes deliverance. The first step for the believer's discipleship is deliverance. Speaking in tongues or the gifts of the Spirit come after deliverance. Today, many believers go after the manifestations of the Spirit (1 Corinthians 12:7-10) and forsake the deliverance of their souls. Many believers who are gifted are struggling in their marriages, education, ministries, families, or careers, simply because they have not dealt with the demonic issues in their lives. You can be gifted but be captive to demons (2 Kings 5:1). Naaman was a mighty man in valour, but he was a leper.

You can be great and a child of God, but you can have spiritual leprosy, meaning that you are afflicted by demons.

> *But there was a certain man, called Simon, which beforetime in the same city used sorcery, and bewitched the people of Samaria, giving out that himself was some great one: To whom they all gave heed, from the least to the greatest, saying, This man is the great power of God. And to him they had regard, because that of long time he had bewitched them with sorceries. But when they believed Philip preaching the things concerning the kingdom of God, and the name of Jesus Christ, they were baptized, both men and women. Then Simon himself believed also: and when he was baptized, he continued with Philip, and wondered, beholding the miracles and signs which were done* (Acts 8:9-13).

> *And when Simon saw that through laying on of the apostles' hands the Holy Ghost was given, he offered them money, Saying, Give me also this power, that on whomsoever I lay hands, he may receive the Holy Ghost* (Acts 8:18-19).

In this scripture, Simeon the sorcerer believed and was baptized (Acts 8:13). He continued with Philip, beholding the signs and wonders done by the apostles. He wanted to purchase the power that the apostles were operating through so that he too could perform the same miracles or make people receive the Holy Spirit by laying hands on them. Simeon is a picture of many Christians who believe, are saved, and are baptized, yet have not gone through the process of deliverance and are going after the gifts of the

Spirit. Many are in the church today who have been saved for many years—20 years, 30 years, or more—and have not gone through any form of deliverance. They want to operate in the gifts of the Spirit, for example, the prophetic ministry or the power gift ministry (healing, faith, or miracles).

The gifts of the Spirit are given to us freely as the Holy Spirit wills (1 Corinthians 12:11). It is possible to operate in the gifts of the Spirit but still be captive to old behaviours, and that alone can deceive people to think they don't need deliverance. Some people have been in the church for a long time, and they do not think that they need deliverance because they operate in the gifts of the Spirit. Every child of God must go through the process of deliverance, and it is the wrong doctrine to think that they do not need it. Deliverance is the first step in the process of discipleship. It is the first thing that must be done before someone moves on to deeper teachings and ministry. This is one of the reasons why believers are struggling in ministry and blaming God for not fulfilling His word in their lives and ministries.

The believer is responsible for knowing that they need deliverance after salvation. Some will argue that they were not taught that theory and they are not open to these teachings, but I will argue that is why we must go back to the basis of our faith. It is like someone who moves from grade one to high school and has missed a significant amount of learning, teaching, and experiences. Accepting this truth is a problem for many believers because they have been Christians for many years and do not see the need for deliverance. The truth is that they are struggling in their Christian walk and are not living a victorious life. There may be many signs of demonization in their lives. Demons will not leave the child of God automatically if they are not confronted. Demons that have invaded the life of the believer before they got saved will not leave automatically because they are now a born-again believer; the demons must be confronted and cast out before they can leave. If they are not commanded and cast out, they will not leave.

Some believers think that because they do not see physical manifestations in their lives, they are free from them. I will argue that the demons do not manifest because no one has confronted them and they are comfortable in the life of the believer. I have seen many people who have come to our services and deliverance clinics to observe, thinking that deliverance is not for them. With these same people, when we start ministering to them and the power of God starts tormenting the demons and they start manifesting in different ways, they are surprised to see that they have such demons in them. Some start hissing like snakes, meowing like cats, and barking like dogs, while others can be violent, scream, and vomit strange substances. I have seen prideful believers despise those who the Holy Spirit was still working on; they chose not to participate. As soon as we ministered to these pride-filled people, many things manifested in them; more than the people they despised.

I encourage everyone not to be super spiritual and think that they do not need deliverance; be wise and humble before God so that you can receive your deliverance.

*Submit yourself therefore to God. Resist the devil, and he will flee from you* (James 4:7).

Deliverance will come when we first submit our lives to God. Therefore humility is the key to our deliverance.

Demons always need an open door to invade the life of the child of God. Luke 11:24 shows that demons can go in and out of people. After they have been cast out of a man, they look for a place to dwell, and if they find none, they return to where they were cast out from. This means demons can re-enter after they are cast out. After we are delivered, we must guard our gates so that we do not open the door for the demons to re-enter our life. We must resist and deny them access into our lives. I have seen believers who were delivered from a demon; they opened the door for them to re-enter and their situation got worse.

> *Then goeth he, and taketh to him **seven** other spirits more wicked than himself; and they enter in, and dwell there: and the last state of that man is worse than the first* (Luke 11:26, emphasis added).

The number seven is a number of perfection and completion, so when the demons re-enter into a life, their situation becomes worse than it was originally and the wickedness of the demons become perfected or complete. After the spirit comes back with seven more spirits, they become eight spirits in total. Eight is the number of new beginning; the state of the individual becomes a new beginning of wickedness. Demons just need a point of contact or an opened door. They only need a crack, not even a big door.

*Neither give place to the devil* (Ephesians 4:27).

If the demons want to re-enter and the door is closed, their access is denied and they can no longer enter into the person.

chapter ten

# DESTINY REPACKAGED

God will rearrange destinies. If destinies are repackaged by Satan, then God will also rearrange destinies that have been repackaged. Satan is the master of repackaging. His assignment is to repackage destinies and lives. John 10:10 says that he comes to steal, to destroy, and to kill. When Satan repackages our destiny, it means that we are not living according to the original plan and purposes of God for our life. Satan finds us to be dangerous when we are blessed by God, and he makes sure that he repackages us to be nothing and to be a curse. We are highly favoured by God, but Satan has repackaged us to be disfavoured. People don't want to be associated with us when we are not what God has created us to be and we become somebody that we are not. Although we have become something else, God is going to rearrange our destiny, and we will live to fulfill our divine purpose. There is no way that the enemy can continue to repackage us.

It is about time that the children of God come out of any satanic repackaging. We must be willing to come out and fulfill God's plans for our lives. We must refuse to be repackaged. We are coming out of shame, reproach, sicknesses, poverty, affliction, and any curses because we are blessed and anointed by God. There is a cause for why we have been repackaged and afflicted for many years. The enemy has done this, and it is the enemy who repackages us. When God created us, He blessed us with favour, peace, joy, righteousness, and liberty. God has blessed man in the beginning. We all should be enjoying the blessings of God.

You are supposed to have children, but you don't. You are supposed to be married by now, but you are not. You are supposed to be finished school by now, but you are not, etc. It is all repackaging. When you are not doing what the Bible says you should be doing, it means you have been repackaged. The Bible says that you are the head and not the tail, but if you are not living this word, you are repackaged. The Bible also says that you will be a lender and not a borrower, so if you are now borrowing, you are repackaged!

*There is an evil which I have seen under the sun, as an error which proceedeth from the ruler: Folly is set in great dignity, and the rich sit in low place. I have seen servants upon horses, and princes walking as servants upon the earth* (Ecclesiastes 10:5-7).

Those who are supposed to be on horses are walking like servants. When someone is riding in your Lexus and you are taking the bus, it is a state of repackaging. You are supposed to be writing cheques for people, but you are not, you are borrowing. Something is wrong!

You know your qualifications, you know your grace and the plans God has concerning your life, but something has gone wrong and you are not living accordingly. There are times when you must be content with whatever situation you find yourself in, but sometimes it is the work of the enemy. You must not accept this repackaging of the enemy.

In Luke 13:11-16, we are introduced to a daughter of Abraham whom Satan had bound with infirmity for 18 years.

*And, behold, there was a woman which had a spirit of infirmity eighteen years, and was bowed together, and could in no wise lift up herself. And when Jesus saw her, he called her to him, and said unto her, Woman, thou art loosed from thine infirmity...And ought not this woman, being a daughter of Abraham, whom Satan hath bound, lo, these eighteen years, be loosed from this bond on the sabbath day?*

The Bible describes her as a daughter of Abraham. She was a child of God who went to the synagogue all the time. She was a seed of Abraham, a covenant child of God like you and me, who had the right to the blessings and inheritance of God, but she was denied of her blessings and had been repackaged in sickness for 18 years.

Don't be comfortable with your repackaged condition. You need the power of the Holy Ghost to destroy witchcraft powers and satanic yokes of repackaging. The power of God will destroy any repackaging situation in your life, ministry, marriage, and finances.

*There is an evil which I have seen under the sun, as an error which proceedeth from the ruler: Folly is set in great dignity, and the rich sit in low place. I have seen servants upon horses, and princes walking as servants upon the earth* (Ecclesiastes 10:5-7).

The rich sit in low places, if you are in a low place and you are not living in abundance, then it is an error and the error must be corrected. It is a mistake for you to be in lack. How can you be a child of the God who created the whole earth and be in lack? It is a mistake! How can you be a child of the Healer and you are sick? It is a mistake. How can servants be riding on horses while princes who are supposed to be riding are walking? Something is wrong; it is a mistake and God has to rearrange your destiny.

Esau was repackaged. He was the one who was supposed to receive the inheritance of his father. He was repackaged and gave his birthright to his brother because of his fleshly desires. He was the cause of his repackaging. There is always a legal right. When we don't appreciate the blessings of God, they will be taken from us.

The enemy is in the business of repackaging destinies. Joseph's brothers repackaged him and sold him to the Egyptians so that he wouldn't become what God had created him to be, but God rearranged his destiny and he fulfilled his destiny. I declare that whatever has held you captive to hinder your destiny is broken, and you will be free to fulfill your destiny. They can try to repackage you, but your dream is still alive. They can put you in a prison, but you will come out and get to your palace. God will make sure that he will bring you out. Don't let the devil deceive you; he is a liar. If you are somewhere that does not represent the will of God for your life, don't accept it; it is a mistake and it must be corrected. The woman we saw in Luke 13 was repackaged, but God set her free to become the woman He created her to be. She was healed by the power of Christ.

Let's look at the story of the prodigal son in Luke 15:11-23.

*And he said, A certain man had two sons: And the younger of them said to his father, Father, give me the portion of goods that falleth to me. And he divided unto them his living. And not many days after the younger son gathered all together, and took his journey into a far country, and there wasted his substance with riotous living. And when he had spent all, there arose a mighty famine in that land; and he began to be in want. And he went and joined himself to a citizen of that country; and he sent him into his fields to feed swine. And he would fain have filled his belly with the husks that the swine did eat: and no man gave unto him.*

*And when he came to himself, he said, How many hired servants of my fathers have bread enough and to spare, and I perish with hunger! I will arise and go to my father, and will say unto him, Father, I have sinned against heaven, and before thee, And am no more worthy to be called thy son: make me as one of thy hired servants.*

*And he arose, and came to his father. But when he was yet a great way off, his father saw him, and had compassion, and ran, and fell on his neck, and kissed him. And the son said unto him, Father, I have sinned against heaven, and in thy sight, and am no more worthy to be called thy son.*

*But the father said to his servants, Bring forth the best robe, and put it on him; and put a ring on his hand, and shoes on his feet: And bring hither the fatted calf, and kill it; and let us eat, and be merry.*

The prodigal son is a picture of a repackaging. He was living in abundance and he demanded his inheritance (which was to be given to him when the father died). This was a wrong demand. The Bible says that he went far away.

When you move out of your set place, you will die because you are out of the will of God and you are far from God and from righteousness; far from your home and your purpose in life. You are opposite of your calling. The prodigal son was eating with swine. He was far from blessings, love, and favour. He was repackaged.

When you are repackaged, you lose everything; you lose your identity and degrade yourself to the lowest point in life. This is what the scripture describes in Ecclesiastes 10; here is a prince who is supposed to be riding on horses, but he is now eating with swine. The Bible says that no man gave to the prodigal son. When you are repackaged, you are rejected, disfavoured, and isolated. People will not favour you because you have been repackaged by the enemy and there is no oil on you; your face is dry. A servant who is not qualified will take your place. It is an error.

You must come to your senses and know who you are. The prodigal son came to himself and decided to go back to his father's house. You have a heavenly Father, who is Jehovah Jireh and will provide all your needs; go back to your Father. Come to your senses so that you can be above the works of Satan. You must make a decision that you are tired of your condition and know who you are in Christ. Declare that you are out of poverty, out of shame, out of sicknesses; you are coming out of the repackaging. When the prodigal son came to himself, he came out of his situation and realized that he must go back to his father's house, his original state, because in his father's house there was abundance.

Take back your inheritance, take back your blessings. It doesn't matter how long you have been repackaged; your future is great.

If you don't acknowledge that you have been repacked, you can never come out of the situation. The Bible says the prodigal son arose and went back. Nobody will correct the mistake for you; you must arise. He identified his situation and arose to correct the mistake. His father was waiting for his son to come back home. God is waiting for you to step into your blessings. Today, you will arise to tap into your blessings and fulfill your destiny. Before you tap into your blessings, you must arise and destroy the repackaging over your life.

chapter eleven

# THE HELMET OF SALVATION

The *helmet* of salvation is very important in spiritual warfare because it protects our minds!

Your head is very important, because if you don't protect your head or if your head is cut off, you die! That's why in Genesis 3:15, when the head of the serpent is bruised, that means the end of Satan. He was defeated on the cross.

That was a prophetic word of God: that there would be a day that the seed of the woman, who would come in the person of Christ, the Messiah; that He would die on the cross; and that by His death, He bruised the head of Satan, that dragon, that serpent, and that leviathan's head.

The one who has been stealing from you.

The one who has been taking from you.

The one that has been afflicting you.

The one who has been oppressing you.

The one who has been causing confusion in your home; bringing sickness and curses. On the cross his head was bruised!

Thankfully because of that, now you have access to what we call the helmet of salvation.

Today as you have the helmet of salvation on, you are protected, your victory is secured, your deliverance, healing, money, and blessing is secured. All the promises of God are secured.

Your salvation has no end because Christ Jesus paid the price and defeated that serpent, Satan, on the cross. Now you are saved, sanctified, forgiven, and have received mercy so no one can take it from you.

Romans 8:30 said that nothing can separate you from the love of God.

Romans 8:35 says that tribulation cannot separate you; death cannot separate you; famine cannot separate you. Nothing can separate you. The only thing that can separate you is *you*!

I will not separate myself from the love of God.

I will not go back to the world.

I will not go back to the kingdom of darkness.

I will not go back to my old life.

I will not go back to Egypt.

I will not go back to the world, because I know that my Saviour has redeemed me and my salvation is eternal.

Your victory is eternal! Sometimes Christians today are up and give a testimony in church, and tomorrow they are down and discouraged. Are you not the person who testified yesterday that God is good? Is this not the same person who was praising God and shouting and clapping hands? What happened?

Child of God, your victory is not up and down; it comes and stays and is forever. I decree permanent victory, healing, and permanent deliverance.

You have victory over the works of the enemy, but now you're afraid that the devil will come again. Understand that the devil will come again, but be not afraid of the devil because he was defeated on the cross forever and has no place in your life.

Some people are afraid even to testify in church because they believe that when they testify, the devil will steal their testimony away. The Bible says that you overcome the devil by the blood of the Lamb and by the word of your testimony (Revelation 12:11). You must declare your testimony when you have the signal in your spirit that it is the time to testify. Everybody has to know what the Lord has done for you, and you must put the devil to shame.

People don't understand my rationale when I take the mic and say, "Give the Lord praise and put the devil to shame." I have to praise God. I have to give all the glory to Him for the opportunity He has given to me. I have to bless His name, and I have to put the devil to shame, because anytime I praise God, I'm putting the devil to shame!

You must walk in power, dominion, and favour. When you wear the helmet of salvation, you are walking in victory and you are demonstrating that you are not ashamed of the gospel of Jesus Christ.

When you see my helmet, you know that Jesus died for me and gave me victory. You automatically know my identity in Christ, and you know that I am walking in victory.

The helmet also protects and covers our minds. In the ancient days, whenever the Roman soldiers fought in warfare without helmets, they ran the risk of being exposed and the enemy cutting off their heads. To protect themselves, the Roman soldiers rode on horses and in chariots, with sharp swords that were approximately four feet long. The Roman soldiers were sure to cover every part of their heads, leaving only small spaces for their eyes and mouths. That is the helmet of salvation! When you put on the helmet of salvation, you are protected, your mind is covered, and you are declaring that Christ is your covering.

Christ is the one who protects your mind from the bruises of the world and the attacks and schemes of Satan to influence you to engage in behaviours that do not please God, so that you will be out of the will of God. If you are not in alignment with God's will, you cannot possibly receive the full blessings of God. You cannot receive double for your shame. If you are not in alignment, you cannot become the person God has created you to be, so the enemy always ensures that you don't put on this valuable helmet of salvation! The breastplate covers your heart, but the mind is a battlefield of spiritual warfare. If the enemy is able to take over and overcome your mind, you will perish.

While undergoing the process of deliverance, ministers may focus on finding a witchcraft spirit to cast out; meanwhile the battle is taking place in the mind of the person being afflicted.

*For as he thinketh in his heart, so is he: Eat and drink, saith he to thee; but his heart is not with thee* (Proverbs 23:7).

The way we think is very important. Our thinking can either contribute to the success of our lives or it can bring total destruction to our lives. The way we think has been shaped by our backgrounds, and by the way in which we were brought up. Since our birth, some of us have experienced negative and inferior words being spoken into our lives and taught to us by our parents. These negative words and thought patterns have built a stronghold in our minds. Even though we are believers today, these strongholds are still contending against us. Even though God says we are the head, we still thinking and behaving like we are the tail.

God said you are the head! God said you are blessed! God said you are healed, but you are still behaving like somebody that is still sick and that is still broken! At times because of the condition of your mind, you are still not well and you are not in the place of experiencing the full blessings of God. In order for you to be blessed, you have to change your way of thinking.

The devil is the source of all evil, but some of the issues you are dealing with are in your mind. If you are able to win in your mind, your deliverance will be expedited and you won't need to desperately seek a prophetic word. At times your mind has been conditioned to always get a prophetic word, and if you don't get a prophetic word, you are upset. I believe a prophetic word without deliverance is not a true prophetic word, because after the Lord has revealed it, there shall be deliverance. If you reveal someone's problem and you cannot help them, it's better not to. But we declare the prophetic word of God and we help through the process of deliverance. As a result of that, we have many tangible testimonies in our ministry.

We need somebody who can speak the mind of God, reveal the counsel of God, and bring us out so that we can escape the traps of the devil. The mind has been programmed that we need a word. On the other hand, we are also shifting our faith from God unconsciously by needing a prophetic word. If we study scripture carefully, we will realize that God doesn't speak to the prophet every time.

In the Old Testament, when God spoke, people typically did not want to hear His prophetic word, because when He spoke, it brought on the fear of God. When Moses stepped in town or when Elijah stepped in town, everybody would flee from the word. Today, people run after prophetic words and have no sense of reverence of God, even if they are living in sin.

I believe in the prophetic word of God. The problem is not always the prophet. The problem is sometimes *the people*. So because of that, we are not benefitting from what God is giving to the church; the gift of prophecy!

Our minds have been clouded and have been bombarded with negative thoughts and negative words. Many times we have received words, and these words made us form a pattern of thought or have a thought system that is not according to the will of God, but Satan has made us believe it's God. Even though you are a child of God, Satan can still put thoughts in your mind and make you think it's God.

*And Satan stood up against Israel, and provoked David to number Israel* (1 Chronicles 21:1).

So David was numbering Israel, and he thought it was of God. The Bible says that it was Satan that stood against the people of God, and then he influenced David, the king, to number the people of God to be out of alignment. David thought it was the mind of God, but in fact it was Satan.

Satan also influences the minds of the children of God. If we don't have the helmet of salvation on, Satan can influence our minds and we can think we are in the will of God. That is why some people can say, "God says this," and tomorrow you see disaster because it wasn't God in the first place.

Some of us today have been afflicted because Satan had a foothold in our minds and established a stronghold. Child of God, I want you to know that it doesn't matter what foothold Satan has gained over your mind, the stronghold shall be pulled down. By the fire of the Spirit of God, we will burn this stronghold into ashes in the name of Jesus Christ. Your mind will be set free today so that you can be what God says you are, so that you can receive the blessings of God and possess your possessions and inheritance. You can have all that God says that you can have and nothing can stop you!

When we talk about spiritual warfare, some people think about the warfare in the Book of Revelation and think about dragons and having nightmares. Spiritual warfare is much more than that! Spiritual warfare is around us all the time, everywhere we go. Our spiritual battle is in our mind! Today, if we can overcome Satan's afflictions in our mind, we will have victory!

The Bible says in the Book of Mark chapter 5 that there was a man who was afflicted. He had a legion of demons, and the Bible said he was out of his mind. He left all his family members, including his mother, father, and children and was sleeping among the tombs. Nobody could tame him; they could not even tie him with a chain. This is because there were spirits in him that had strong influence on his mind and afflicted him. He could not sleep, just like some of us today cannot sleep because we have spirits and thoughts contending against our minds.

If we can renew our minds today and banish negative self-talk about the many aspects of our life and cast that devil out of our minds today, there will be total transformation. The battle is in our mind.

Understand that there is a difference between bondage and captivity. When you are a child of God, you are out of slavery and you are not in bondage. If you are a child of God, you can be saved. You can be out of the world, just like Israel was out of Egypt, but they were bound through the captivity of their minds.

You can be saved, but your mind can be in captivity! Your mind can be captive to poverty; you can be captive to sin; you can be captive to curses; you can be captive to oppression; you can be captive to all evil. I want you to know that God's purpose and plans for your life are not evil. His plans are good, and they have an expected end (Jeremiah 29:11)! You have a great future. God has you in mind, and He wants you to prosper.

Speak these declarations into your life today: You are the head, not the tail! You are blessed when you go out! You are blessed when you come in! You are highly favoured by God! You are blessed by God. You are a child of God. You are the son/daughter of God. You are sanctified by God. You are filled with the Holy Ghost. You are born of the Spirit of God! You are the anointed of the Lord. You are seated together in heavenly places in Christ Jesus.

It doesn't matter how anointed you are, you can still be bound in your mind, because the anointing is a free gift given to you by God! However, in order to loose your mind from being bound, you have to do it yourself, not God!

Some people are cursing God and asking, "God, why is this person blessed and that person is not blessed?" You can actually do all things through Christ Jesus. That is the mindset we should have. Always tell yourself, "*I know I can do all things* through Christ Jesus who strengthens me; there is nothing I set my mind to do that I cannot do."

Tell yourself, "I'll be what God says that I am. He wishes above all things that I would prosper!" God rejoices in the prosperity of His servants. The difference between the person who is struggling in life and the person who has broken through is the mind.

The Bible talks about renewing our mind and says that as a man thinks in his heart, so is he. Using this scripture as a model and applying wisdom, it is safe to conclude that with the battles we fight, we cannot blame God. We must accept responsibility and admit that some delays in our lives are caused by the activities of our minds.

The Bible says that when Daniel prayed, immediately God released answers! There was a demonic interference of the manifestation of his answered prayers. Bear in mind that sometimes there are interferences and delays! Some are not necessarily demonic delays, but simply the state of our minds. It's your mind that is delaying your husband and your wife. It's your mind that is delaying your house or your baby. Immediately when you change your mind, things will also change.

Spiritual battles are born in the mind. The mind is so important that when David killed Goliath, the Bible says David beheaded Goliath after striking him with the stone, to declare total victory.

Today, when fighting the attacks of the enemy, ensure that you don't simply kill the enemy; take charge and cut off the head of that serpent! The head symbolizes absolute victory, completion, and perfection.

When God instructed Saul to destroy all the Amalekites, he refused, left the king alive, and the good spoils of the land. You are not to have mercy on the enemy. Remember to maximize any opportunities that God has given you over your enemies. Take your deliverance now and recover everything that the enemy has stolen from you.

As opposed to experiencing total deliverance, some people are satisfied with half deliverance. Pharaoh said in Exodus 8:28, "I will let you go, but don't go far!" This is still true in the lives of some believers. They have gone but have not gone far. Whenever the devil wants them, he gains easy access to them, and that is because they have not completely cut the devil off from all aspects of their lives. As result, he still has ties to their ministries, homes, marriages, and finances and must be promptly cut off!

When you put on the helmet of salvation, you receive revelation knowledge. God opens your spiritual eyes, to have insight of His Word. He also blocks the enemy from contaminating your mind. Your mind has to be renewed to know that the devil you are fighting against has been defeated.

The Bible talks about man having three dimensions, which are the spirit, soul, and body. It's similar to the mysteries of God, with the Trinity, Father, Son, and Holy Spirit. God is not three, but God is one! You cannot understand it physically or mathematically; it's a mystery, and it must be revealed to us by the Holy Spirit. Trying to apply a mathematical equation or logics to this mystery will prove to be futile as the concept is not of the world and doesn't make sense to our natural minds.

Just as God is one, man is one, not three! According to 1 Thessalonians 5:23, man has a spirit, soul, and body.

*And the very God of peace sanctify you wholly; and I pray God your whole spirit and soul and body be preserved blameless unto the coming of our Lord Jesus Christ* (1 Thessalonians 5:23).

The Spirit lives forever, and the spirit man is created in the image of God. God breathed into our nostrils, and man became a living soul, according to Genesis 2:7.

The Bible says that God so loved the world that he gave His only begotten Son to the world, so if anyone believes in Him, he will not die, but will have *everlasting life*. So your spirit man lives forever if you believe in Christ Jesus.

Now you have a soul, and your soul has five components, which are the mind, the will, the imagination, the emotions, and the intellect. As we are dealing with the helmet of salvation, it is important for us to focus on the mind. The mind also has three components that God uses to bring His purposes to pass:

- The conscious mind
- The subconscious mind
- The conscience.

God works through the stages of what He has already created man to be. Therefore, man cannot automatically be successful. It's more than saying I'm blessed. God has a system for us to be progressive and blessed, and this all deals with the mind.

It's our spirit that knows God, but through our minds we express our emotions to God and use our minds to reason. Some people think that when we become born again, we have to put the mind aside, and that is a lie of the devil! We walk in the spirit, not in the flesh, but we also have to be reasonable people and think! God has given us the mind to think critically, according to His purpose and His plans for our lives.

The conscious mind is the stage where our day-to-day decision making occurs. So every day, the decisions we make comes from our conscious mind.

As you are reading this book, I believe you are making decisions. This means that you are a reasonable person as you are actually thinking.

The subconscious gets into your conscious mind and automatically brings out what it has already recorded. As you go through your daily life, you naturally react to things based on the things that were previously established in your thought system. With the subconscious, the things that you were brought up with or taught remain as a factor of your thought process. You could have been taught that you cannot be healed, and this is in your mind. At times with your subconscious, when it's time for healing, the thought comes out that healing is not for you.

Your conscience is the part of your mind that you use to judge things, and that establishes your belief system. The information learned and things you have gone through in life, including experiences and things that were passed on to you by parents and even by churches, made you establish a belief system that is not in line with God's will. Having this wrong belief system hinders you from moving to the next dimension in your life, but if you can pull it down today, you can break through! You can get to the place where you receive a double blessing for all of your shame and the affliction that you have faced.

*And they went and came to Moses, and to Aaron, and to all the congregation of the children of Israel, unto the wilderness of Paran, to Kadesh; and brought back word unto them, and unto all the congregation, and shewed them the fruit of the land* (Numbers 13:26).

The Bible says that the children of Israel were in the wilderness and they sent spies into the promised land. God had promised them a land, and the purpose of them coming out of Egypt was to come out of bondage and to have relationship with their God, the God of Abraham. The children of Israel went through the wilderness, and it took them forty years—a trip that was supposed to only take them a few days. The reason for that is because of the mind. It's not because of the giants, because God knew that the giants were already there.

The problems you are having now are not because of the demons, they are because of your mind. God knew that the demons were already there before He saved you. God said you are blessed regardless of which devil, what spirit, what power—your mind is the culprit of your problems.

So the Bible says that the children of Israel sent twelve men from each tribe to spy out the land, and they brought back bad or evil reports. The interesting thing here is that when they returned, they admitted that what God had told them about the land was true. They brought the fruit of the land and held it as evidence. That proves that God's word is true.

God *will never lie to you*. Though the children of Israel had physical evidence of God's promise to them, their minds were still not changed. For some of us, regardless of what God does, our minds will remain unchanged.

The children of Israel saw the fruit, yet had the same mind. They said, "We are not able, what God said is true!" In a nutshell, the battle was in their minds. They saw that the giants were greater than them. They saw that they couldn't defeat the giants, and they saw that they could not possess their land. The problem that they were dealing with started from when they were back in Egypt, because of what was put in their minds—their thought system, which could not be changed in one day.

When we look at ourselves today as born-again believers, even though we may speak in tongues and may be gifted and anointed, there is a stronghold of the enemy in our minds. This stronghold in our minds limits us and pulls us down, telling us that despite the evidence of God's blessing, we cannot receive the blessings of God; nor can we possess and walk in victory.

God said in the book of Numbers, "I cannot do business with these people! All the numbered men have to die!" We cannot be held captive in our mind and possess the promise of God. We have built a thought system that does not believe in the promise of God. We say it, but we don't live it! You can cast out devils from people and they can manifest and do everything, but if the mindset stays the same, they cannot experience total deliverance.

For some people, it's so easy for them to get their breakthrough; however for some others, it's not so easy due to their mindset!

Before the children of Israel came out of Egypt, they were slaves. They were supposed to be great, but the Egyptians oppressed them, so they had that slave mentality imprinted on their minds. That is a stronghold! How could a slave go and fight a giant, even though they knew about the giant's history; they were sons of Anak. The children of Israel couldn't fathom how they would be able to go and fight against these giants. It's the mind! For us believers, if you just renew your mind, any giant in your life, any Goliath in your life, any sons of Anak in your life can be defeated today. Children of God, it doesn't matter what spirit is contending against you; there is no power of darkness or problem that you cannot overcome. With the mindset of victory and the helmet of salvation, you will definitely overcome it all!

In Mark 5:9, Jesus asked the man with an unclean spirit, "What is your name?" and he said "Legions!" Jesus had a reason for asking. Whenever the demons wanted to talk, typically Jesus rebuked them, but this time he didn't rebuke them. When demons started to reveal Jesus' identity as the Son of God, He rebuked the demons, because demons are liars. Jesus didn't need the demons to identify Him or praise Him or tell Him who He was; Jesus knew who He was! However, in this passage of scripture, Jesus asked the demons what their name was and they responded "legions," for they were many. That means thousands of demons held that man captive in his mind. Why would demons be interested in one man? You will find out when you study the scriptures: after his deliverance, the bound man became one of the greatest evangelists in those days.

The devil wants to hold your mind captive to prevent you from walking in freedom to become the person that

God wants you to be. God will use you as an instrument, just like the man bound by legions, and many are depending on you for their deliverance, for their healing, for their breakthrough, so He is interested in only your destiny.

That is why you are facing challenges; that is why you are being tormented and harassed by the devil, not because you have done anything wrong, but because of your future, because of the hand of God upon your life. That is why the devil is afflicting you. Thank God that the Son of God was made manifest to destroy the works of the devil, that you can be free and walk in victory, that the plans of God for your life will be fulfilled.

I therefore command you right now to fulfill your destiny and experience the blessings of God!

Joseph told his brothers about his dream, and they didn't understand. They wanted to kill him because of wickedness in their minds that caused them to be jealous of Joseph's dreams and destiny.

God's will for your life is great. The devil's plan for your life is to stop you from becoming great. If you can change your mind and put on the helmet of salvation, you will defeat all spirits that are contending against your destiny. Child of God, though these spirits harass you daily, don't give up on God, because God has not given up on you! Let nothing separate you from the love of God. Let no famine, let no poverty or affliction separate you, for God loves you!

> *And Joseph said unto them, Fear not: for am I in the place of God? But as for you, ye thought evil against me; but God meant it unto good, to bring to pass, as it is this day, to save much people alive* (Genesis 50:19-20).

For what man has meant for evil, to afflict you with their wicked imaginations, will not be fulfilled, nor will it prevail. Let them gather together and think evil. Let them think that even God is not with you, because you have not yet seen the promises of God come to pass in your life.

Deep within, you know that God's word will surely come to pass as He cannot *lie* to you. Some may look at you and laugh at you today, and say, "Where is your God?" Tell them to wait until tomorrow so that they can see *God's word come to pass.*

Think of Joseph who was promoted to Pharoah's right hand, after all of the evil that his brothers did to him. God turned it around for good. With any evil that comes to you, don't curse your affliction, don't curse your persecution, and don't curse your enemies, because God is using these trials to bring to pass His perfect will.

I thank God for my enemies! If they had not persecuted me and lied to me, I would not be where I am. Thank God for the lives of your enemies and pray for them to live and not die. For God said that He will prepare a table before you in the presence of your enemies. Don't let today's problems determine your tomorrow. Never allow your circumstance today to stop you from going forward, but because God is with you, He is setting you up for a blessing.

*And be not conformed to this world: but be ye transformed by the renewing of your mind, that ye may prove what is that good, and acceptable, and perfect, will of God* (Romans 12:2).

You have to be transformed by the renewing of the mind. We were saved; we came from Egypt; we came from the world (Egypt stands for the world); and now we are in the Kingdom of God, but we brought a lot of baggage from the world. We used to think according to the world's system, so Apostle Paul addressed the children of God in Rome and told them they had to change their way of thinking. Even for a born-again believer, change does not occur right away. That's why some people still behave the same way that they used to behave when they were in the world. They think that when they are born again, everything automatically changes.

The truth of the matter is that I have not met anybody in the Body of Christ that is perfect! I've dealt with many wonderful people who are honest and holy people of God, but the truth is that everybody has still some world in them.

That is why it's important for us to go through the process of deliverance. Deliverance is not just about casting out witches. There are behaviours in us that are demonic. With some of the demonic behaviours demonstrated in the church, people will make excuses for those behaviours, saying, "This is just how I am." Now just because you've lived that way and that is how you think, does not mean that is how you are meant to be!

You were not created by God to be that way. Therefore, it's your duty to go through the process of transformation, and that happens by the renewing of the mind. This means the word of God is the standard to guide your mind and the decisions you make.

There is a difference between memorizing scripture and acting on the word of God. Some people have the ability to memorize scripture and literally know almost all of the scriptures! However, if you look at their lifestyle, you may see no truth and they are not walking in power and glory. So clearly, it's more than reciting and memorizing scripture. It is the application of scripture in your daily life and living by the word that transforms you!

If the Bible says don't steal, then you stop stealing. You are moved from being a thief to someone who doesn't steal, and now gives to others. That is the renewal of the mind!

Let's go back to the three aspects of the mind: the conscience, the conscious mind, and the subconscious mind.

The conscious mind is now changing your way of thinking with your awareness of new things, but your subconscious mind, being the part of your mind that recalls things, will pick up what you have now started doing by not stealing. As a result, every time that you have an opportunity to steal, you will not steal again, because the subconscious part of your mind has been changed. This forms your conscience, which is your judgment, and now you don't steal.

Your belief system being changed and becoming a way of life is what will make you live a victorious Christian life! So you see, it's more than just reciting scripture, it's about applying it and changing your way of thinking.

If you want to be successful from today onwards, it can happen. The decision you make today will start establishing a new thought system in you and will become a belief system that you will live by. That is what will make you possess the blessings of God. You will receive your deliverance and overcome all giants. Your language will change from saying "I am not able" to "I *am able*!"

Perhaps you've been struggling in your mind, and your thought system has affected your core. It has affected the blessings of God. This thought system could have altered how you look at yourself and that which God says you are.

In the book of Luke chapter 8, the Bible says there was a blind man. This blind man heard that Jesus was in town, and he cried out for mercy because the son of David was the Messiah and the Messiah was able to make the blind see. So he had a revelation and he changed his mind. The Bible says that immediately when the people tried to stop him from shouting, the louder he shouted. Don't let anybody stop you from becoming what God wants you to be! The Bible said Jesus heard because he did not hold his peace.

The Bible said that the blind man removed his garment when he was called by Jesus. This garment symbolized his status as a beggar. Not only was he blind, he was a beggar. The first thing he did to show his shift in thinking was to remove his garment. He moved from being a beggar to being someone who received mercy and was healed. His status changed because he renewed his mind and had an encounter with the Messiah, the Son of David.

Right now, the garments of shame, reproach, sin, poverty, bondage, and captivity must be thrown away. This symbolizes your change of mind and the change of your position. Change the way of thinking and the way of making decisions. Change your belief system. In order for you to see the promise of God come to pass in your life, you have to reposition your thinking. It's more than hands being laid on you or prayers. Make this declaration now:

*In the name of Jesus Christ, I declare I'm a child of God. I declare I'm a servant of God. I declare I'm born of the Spirit of God. I declare I'm seated together in heavenly places in Christ Jesus. I declare today is my day of deliverance. I declare today is my acceptable day. It is my day of freedom! It is my day of liberation. In the name of Jesus, I yield my spirit; I yield my mind to the Spirit of God. I pull down any negative thoughts established in my mind. Today, I destroy by the fire of the Holy Ghost any foothold that Satan has gained in my mind; in the name of Jesus Christ! I declare that I will think about things that are true, honest, just, pure, lovely, and of good-report.*

chapter twelve

# VICTORIOUS CHRISTIAN LIFE

We must live a victorious Christian life. We are not defeated, but we are victorious people of God. Victory is our name. We always live and walk in victory and in power. There is no way that we can be defeated because victory has already been secured on the cross by Jesus Christ, the captain of our warfare and the Good Shepherd. We have many shepherds, but Jesus Christ is the Good Shepherd and the invisible Shepherd. We thank God for all that He did for us on the cross.

We should not be downtrodden and defeated by the pressures of this world and the activities of Satan. Satan will do everything to afflict us so that we will not fulfill our destiny. He will try to steal from us, take from us, discourage us, and bring oppression and depression, even though we are children of God. Even though victory has been secured for us, we are not all walking in victory and we are living below our potential. We must always remember that we have been anointed and called by God to live a victorious life. We can only live a victorious life because of what has been done on the cross for us. The cross is not the destination of Jesus; rather it was a transition. Jesus went to the cross and defeated the enemy. His destination was going back to where He came from;

evidence being that the Bible says that Jesus is seated at the right hand of God, interceding for the child of God (Romans 8:34). He has given us the Holy Spirit to help us to live a victorious Christian life. Every believer must understand the importance of the work done on the cross and the power on the cross. The power is not on the wooden or the physical cross that you see, but the work done on the cross is that which produces the power. Satan was defeated. Colossians 2:15 talks about how he was put to shame. Jesus Christ put him to shame and disgraced him openly. The child of God today can celebrate because of what was done for us on the cross!

Without the cross, there would not be resurrection. The cross had to come before the resurrection. You must die before you are resurrected. So Jesus Christ died. When you die, typically you are buried. Jesus Christ was placed in the tomb, however He was resurrected. All the prophets of old died and none were resurrected. Only Jesus Christ died and was resurrected. That proved that He is the true son of David, the Messiah. Behold the Lamb of God that taketh away the sin of this world (John 1:29). Not the sins, but the sin in a singular tense, the actual nature of sin.

Jesus took the nature of sin. The sin of Adam that was transferred to human beings is the root of all the problems we face today. The solution to the problem of man is the cross, and Jesus Christ came and gave us the answer. He delivered us through the work He did on the cross, where He defeated the nature of sin. Whether we like it or not, everyone that comes into this world comes with sin. When Jesus Christ came, He defeated the power of darkness. The nature of sin was destroyed so that today as we believe that

Jesus Christ was raised from the dead, we know that we too can receive the life of God.

We died to sin and now have been resurrected to live a new life and walk in power. That same Spirit that raised Christ from the dead dwells in us, and He shall quicken our mortal body so that we can be above the nature of sin. We are not going return to sin, but we'll walk in righteousness by the Spirit of God that helps us to live a holy life. Today we are privileged and blessed to have the Holy Spirit. The Holy Spirit is with us to help us live a victorious Christian life free from bondage.

All of the promises of God and the blessings of God are tied to the cross. Before we can walk in victory and live a victorious Christian life, there are three very important things that we have to understand:

- First of all, we have to understand the work done on the cross.
- Next we have to understand the principles of faith in Christ.
- Finally, we have to understand why the Holy Spirit came.

If you understand and you live by these things, you will always be above the works of the enemy. Even though the devil will bring things against you, you will not be shaken because you understand what was done on the cross—he was defeated. Satan cannot lie to you. He can't take your blessing. He can't take your favour. He can't take your children, your money, your business, or your health. Satan can't take that which God has given to you because he was defeated on the cross. Therefore, when he comes to steal from you, he is just lying to you. Turn to the devil and tell him that he is a liar! When he brings sickness to you, tell him, "You are a liar!" When he brings oppression, tell him, "You are a liar!" When he wants to put you down, tell him, "You are a liar!" When he tries to do anything, you must remind him that he is a liar, because that is not the truth of God's word. Satan comes to lie to you, to prevent you from succeeding. He comes to lie to you and tell you that you are still a sinner. You were saved and you are saved, but Satan tells you that you are still living in sin even though you are no more a sinner! The handwriting of ordinances that is against you has been blotted away.

> *Blotting out the handwriting of ordinances that was against us, which was contrary to us, and took it out of the way, nailing it to his cross* (Colossians 2:14).

Sin simply means missing the mark. After man sinned in the beginning, every time man aspires to do right or wants to try by his might to reach God or be righteous, he always misses the mark. Your best cannot make you righteous. Doing good works cannot make you righteous. So every time you try to do the right thing, you still miss the mark and fall short. That is why it was imperative and important for Jesus Christ to come and pay the price on the cross for you, because you cannot save yourself. You cannot save your life; it is by the work done on the cross! If you understand the mysteries of the cross, you will know that while Jesus had no sin, He took your place of sin on the cross so that you can receive His righteousness (2 Corinthians 5:21).

You are saved not by your works, according to Ephesians, but you are saved by grace through faith. You can't buy your salvation regardless how much money you have. Money cannot buy your salvation. You cannot buy righteousness as it is by the grace of God. Stop depending on your own strength and abilities. Stop depending on what you can do and what you cannot do and know that it's by the grace of God. Jesus died for you so that today, by faith, you can live a holy life. The power of the work done on the cross allows us to see the demonstration of the love of God to us.

If all men have rejected you, if a father or a mother has rejected you, God is a father to you and He loves you. His Son died on the cross—that alone settles the matter. There is one who loves you above everyone—God, and He's your Father! For God so loved the world that He sent His Son, Jesus, His only begotten Son who took your place. He expressed and demonstrated His love to you. You have to understand that the cross has so much to offer.

The cross brings us together. The enmity between us and God is no more, and because of the cross and the work done, now we have peace with God. We can go to the throne of grace and obtain mercy. This means that when we have problems, we can call upon God. When we are in need, we can call upon God. When we need something, and we are in a crisis, we have somebody to call upon. All men can reject us and refuse to hear our case and our side of the matter. There is somebody called God the Father who can hear our story. He can understand, for He identified Himself with us! He is a man of sorrow, according to Isaiah—full of sorrow because of us. He was grieved, He was in pain because of us. There is so much in the cross for us to understand. Just know that because of the cross, we can live a victorious Christian life today.

We know that the powers of darkness in our bloodlines have been destroyed because of the cross, and we know that every power of darkness that comes against us has been defeated. We have power over sickness, poverty, shame, reproach, oppression, and affliction, all because of the cross! We can defeat everything that the enemy brings against us because of the cross! The cross qualifies us, not our backgrounds.

You can come from a poor family that is cursed and are idol worshippers and sinners, but the cross sanctifies you, cleans you, and forgives you. You are saved by the work done on the cross. The cross gives us that assurance that our destiny is secured. You will by all means succeed. You will by all means prosper. It doesn't matter what any man says. What God's word says concerning your destiny, your family, your children shall come to pass. If God says that you are the head, you will still be the head, and nobody can change your destiny. We abort any spirit that wants to abort your blessing or your destiny. We declare to that spirit, it shall come to pass, and you will be what God says that you are.

No one can cancel the plan of God concerning your life. That which the word of God says you are you will always be. You are healed of God because of the blood of Jesus, and you are curse-free because of the curse that was placed on Jesus Christ. Now you can receive the blessings of Abraham. You have to understand these principles, then you can walk in victory. When you are walking, you are walking with your head lifted up, and you know that you are walking in victory. You are walking in power. You will not let the circumstances and the activities of the enemy dictate to you who you are. You dictate to the situation. You speak to the situation. You let the situation know who you are. You let the devil know that he was defeated. You remind him in case he forgets that he is defeated. You want to remind him. He tried to mess with your life, but he has been defeated a long time. You don't have to fight for any victory today. You are fighting from the position of victory. Victorious people fight from the position of victory. They don't fight for victory.

The Apostle Paul said in 1 Corinthians 1:23, *"But we preach Christ crucified, unto the Jews a stumbling block, and unto the Greeks foolishness."* He said we preach Christ crucified. We preach Him who is crucified. We don't preach about ourselves. We don't preach about what we have and what we don't have. It's all garbage when we hear people boasting and telling us what they have and don't have. When we turn on the TV and hear people preaching about the cars, houses, and airplanes that they have, we turn it off! We preach Christ crucified. That is what we need. All those things are vanity, and they are things to serve us.

Don't get me wrong. I believe in good things. But I don't have to preach about material things. Cars will not make me live a victorious life, nor will houses make me live a victorious life. Nobody dies and carries a plane or car to heaven. Nobody takes anything there! The silver and gold belong to God. God created everything, and everything in this earth belongs to God. So if God blesses you with a material thing, just thank God for it. Be certain not to make your material possessions your god. They shouldn't be everything for you. Christ crucified is the most important thing. He was crucified so that today we can walk in victory.

The next thing is understanding biblical faith or understanding the principles of faith. We need faith to be successful! We have to have faith in the person of Christ, not in things. When we are talking about faith, we are not talking about faith in institutions, denominations, people, churches, or even pastors. We are talking about having faith in one person and that is Jesus Christ. We have faith in Jesus Christ and what He did on the cross. Our faith is not in men. Our faith is not in systems. Our faith is not in money. Our faith is not in houses. Our faith is not in possessions. Our faith is not in material things, for the cross is the object of our faith. Without the cross, we don't have faith. When I'm talking about faith, I'm talking about having faith in what Jesus did. Without faith, Jesus cannot come into our life and we cannot be saved. That is why the Bible says that we are saved by grace through faith.

*For by grace are ye saved through faith; and that not of yourselves: it is the gift of God* (Ephesians 2:8).

You are saved by grace through faith, which is a gift of God, and it's not by your works. God made it easy so that everybody can be saved. It's not complicated. All that you have to do to be saved is to have faith in what was done on the cross for you. Men have tried everything to be saved and to have a good relationship with God, but it all failed. It couldn't work. All the men of old tried, but it couldn't work and that's why the law was given. Even the law didn't help them, as it simply revealed their sins. Consider the ten commandments: if you broke one commandment and obeyed the other nine, then what? Nothing, according to James. Though everybody tried, nobody was able to live according to the law of Moses or to obey the ten commandments. That is why God had to come in the person of His Son Jesus to fulfill the law. Jesus Christ is the fulfillment of the law, and now we have another law that is higher than the law of Moses. That law is the law of the Spirit, according to Romans 8:2, *"For the law of the Spirit of life in Christ Jesus hath made me free."*

Any time we try to do right but cannot, that is the law of sin. However, the law of the Spirit is through Christ Jesus, and it's by His grace. The law of the Spirit gives us freedom; not to do just anything, but freedom in the sense that we are living by the grace of God. It's the grace of God that helps us and empowers us day by day to do the right thing. It's the grace of God that will make us obey the word and principles of God. That being said, it is not a law that we try by our strength. As such, we don't say that "Because I'm righteous I did this" and then look down upon those who didn't do right. If we operate that way, we are operating in the old system, which was the law of Moses. This law revealed the sins of the people in those days, because during that time people who thought that they had studied the law looked down upon those who committed sin.

When the woman caught in adultery was brought to Jesus, He told her accusers that if anyone had no sin, let him cast the first stone. They all started running away. That indicated that all of them had something that they had done wrong. They had broken the law, yet they were crucifying someone. It's by the grace of God. It's by the grace of God. Anyone who is always crucifying people and has no mercy is probably doing something worse than the people they are crucifying. The grace of God does not give us the license to keep on sinning.

*What shall we say then? Shall we continue in sin, that grace may abound? God forbid. How shall we, that are dead to sin, live any longer therein?* (Romans 6:1-2).

You see, we don't have to continue in sin because the nature of sin has been crucified. There is a difference between the nature of sin and the act of sin. The nature of sin has been destroyed by Jesus Christ on the cross, yet sometimes you do lie a little bit. Are you saved? Yes you are saved, but you still lie. You get angry sometimes, and you sin. You hate people sometimes, and you sin. You have envy in your heart, and you sin. It doesn't mean that the nature of sin has not been destroyed. The nature of sin has been destroyed, but sometimes we act in sin. So there are two different things here. The nature of sin has been destroyed, and that means you are no more a sinner. You died with Christ and now you are resurrected. That is what the scripture says. You died with Him and you are baptized with Him! You suffered with Him, but now as Christ rose up from the dead, so are you risen from sin and from the grave. You died to sin, and now you are living a new life.

If you believe in Christ Jesus, your old life is passed away and now you have become a new creature, to live a new life, a holy life. It's not by might or by your power but by the power of the Spirit of God that you live. Now it's the law of the Spirit that helps you. That is why Romans 8:1 says, "Now there is no more condemnation to those who walk not after the flesh but after the Spirit!" There is no more condemnation. No one can condemn you. You are justified by Christ.

So because of your faith in Him, now you are justified. You are justified, and justification deals with you just as if you have not sinned. The just shall live by faith! You are justified, and now your lifestyle has to be the life of faith. There is no way you can be successful without living by faith. Without faith, you can't please God. We don't walk by sight. We walk by faith. For example, the doctor could tell you that you are sick and that they diagnosed a disease. It's a fact, but it's not the truth, as not every fact is the truth. The truth is God's word, and the truth of God's word can cancel the fact of what has been said. It is a fact that this thing is there, but God's word says something different! You stand on God's word as you believe His word. You declare and proclaim God's word. You believe that God's word says that "by his stripes you are healed," and you decree it until you see the manifestation of the healing power of God in your life!

You may not have a job, and you may not have money. Your bank account is sick, it's broke. It's a fact. It's not the truth, but it's a fact that your bank account is running in the red. It's negative. The Bible says that it is God who gives you the power to make wealth. "By faith I believe in the word of God, that I'll make wealth. I'll be successful. Money will work for me! I decree and declare that money will work for me!"

We believe that we have faith in the word of God. Our faith is not in systems. Our faith is not in material things, but our faith is in the word of God. For faith comes by hearing and hearing by the word of God (Romans 10:17)! Faith doesn't come by any other thing. If we want to increase in faith, we have to hear the word over and over.

The Bible said that in the beginning was the word (John 1). And the word was with God. And the word is God. In verse 14 of John 1, the word became flesh. Jesus is the word and He died on the cross for our salvation. If you believe in Him, the word is wrapped up in Him. He is the word. So in order for you to increase in faith, when you believe in the word of God, you must increase in faith! When you increase in faith, it's not in things. It's not in people. It's not in anything. It's in the word of God, and that is why you increase. To live a victorious Christian life, you must increase in faith. You must walk in faith. For things can be against you. Everything can be negative. Everything can be against you, but you are not walking by sight, you are walking by faith. You are not walking by your situation. You are not walking by your feelings. You are not walking by what you hear people say. You are walking and living by what the word of God says. The economy will say that you cannot succeed. People will say you cannot be blessed. People will say many things. You know what the word of God says, and you declare the word of God and you believe in the word of God. Even when all hope is gone, don't give up! The word of God will surely come to pass.

Perhaps you are looking for a husband. You are wanting a baby. You are looking for a blessing. You want to give up as you have done everything that you know. The word of God says that you are blessed with all spiritual blessings (Ephesians 1:3). Your blessing is in the realm of the spirit, and it's taking time to manifest in the physical realm. It takes faith to bring the manifestation of your blessings. It takes faith to bring the blessing of your husband. It takes faith to bring the blessing of that new business. It takes faith to bring the blessing of the manifestation of healing in your body. It shall come to pass! You are already healed by God. Don't hear and respect the lies of the devil and people. God's word says you are blessed, and nothing can change it.

We have faith in His word because with all these things, we don't do it for ourselves. It's for God's work, and God will make sure He'll fulfill His word. So biblical faith is having faith in the person of Jesus. Without faith we cannot please God; faith comes by hearing and hearing by the word of God.

Finally, to be a successful Christian and walk in victory or to live a victorious Christian life, we need the Holy Spirit. We need the Holy Spirit to empower us and to help us. The Bible says that He will send the Holy Spirit to come to help us (John 14:16). The Holy Spirit will come, and the Holy Spirit doesn't work outside the framework of the cross. The Holy Spirit was released, and without the cross, the Holy Spirit will not be released to us. Jesus went to the cross and died. After He ascended to heaven, He sent the Holy Spirit. The Holy Spirit comes to empower us to live a victorious Christian life. The Holy Spirit comes to dwell in us. In our prayer life, the Holy Spirit will help us. The Bible says He leads us. He guides us. He convicts us. We can talk to the Holy Spirit. He has ears. He speaks to us.

The Holy Spirit can help us to achieve everything we need. If we want to be successful in marriage, the Holy Spirit can help us. If we want to be successful in our education, the Holy Spirit will help us. In our work, in our business, in our family life, the Holy Spirit can help us. The Holy Spirit is in us to help us with everything in ministry. We cannot do the ministry of God without the Holy Spirit. The Holy Spirit comes to empower us. After the Holy Spirit has come, He will give us power—power to be witnesses of Him! The Holy Spirit comes and anoints us. We receive the power from above to tread upon serpents, scorpions, and all the works of the enemy.

When the Holy Spirit comes, yokes and curses can be destroyed. When the Holy Spirit comes, any problem that we are dealing with can be destroyed by the reason of the anointing, because we have the power of the Holy Ghost. We need the Holy Spirit to work in our lives in order to be victorious Christians. The Holy Ghost is very important, and God will use us by the Holy Spirit. The Holy Spirit will work through us so that through us others will be blessed. We've become witnesses of Christ, and people will see the power of God in our lives, that we serve a living God, that the God we serve is not dead. If they see us, they will see the blessing of God. If they see us, they will see the glory of God. If they see us, they will see the favour of God upon our life.

The lives of some believers do not encourage others to be Christians; in fact, they can be discouraged to be Christians. On the other hand, some unbelievers can see Christians and want to be just like them. That is being a witness. "Wow, I see something special about this person." They don't understand, but they are seeing the glory of God upon your life. I release the oil of the Spirit of God upon your life; so that people will see the favour and the glory of God upon your life. Wherever you go, they will know that God is with you. God was with Joseph even in prison; the favour of God was still upon his life. I declare that everywhere you go, any situation that you are in, the oil of God and the favour of God will flow upon your life to overcome that situation, because of the oil of the Spirit of God upon you. There is no way to live a victorious life without the oil of the Spirit of God. I decree and declare the anointing of God to be activated in your life, that through the anointing, you'll break through every invisible barrier in your life. You'll leap over every wall of demarcation and every hindrance in your life. You'll be able to overcome it by the anointing of God. You'll run through a troop. Your feet are anointed like hind's feet. The oil of the Spirit of God has anointed you. I decree and declare that you receive speed to overcome; speed to recover; speed to inherit; speed to possess; speed to increase; speed to overcome all your enemies.

It's by the Spirit of God that you can possess your possessions. I declare that today you'll possess every blessing due to you, because of the anointing of the Holy Ghost that is upon your life. Every challenge you are facing, by the anointing of God, you can overcome. You are more than conquerors through Christ Jesus. If there is any challenge in your life that you want to overcome, I pray that God would release that anointing upon you in the name of Jesus Christ.

In the name of Jesus, I pray that the Spirit of God will empower the son and daughter of Abraham! I declare and decree that by the anointing of the Holy Spirit that every yoke in your life be destroyed and you have the upper hand over the works and activities of your enemy. I decree that from today onwards, you walk in victory and see the manifestation of the blessings of God in your life.

chapter thirteen

# TOTAL DELIVERANCE PRAYER POINTS

Thank You, Jesus Christ, the captain of my warfare, for my salvation and total deliverance.

I confess and repent of every sin that I have committed that has opened the door for Satan and his demons to invade my life (1 John 1:9).

I confess and repent of the sins of my ancestors (Daniel 9:8-16; Nehemiah 1:6-9).

I declare that I am forgiven and the handwriting of ordinances that are against me are erased (Colossians 2:14).

I declare I am a child of God and joint heir with Christ Jesus (Romans 8:16-17).

I declare that I am called, justified, and glorified (Romans 8:30).

I declare I am seated in heavenly places together with Christ Jesus (Ephesians 2:6).

I break and destroy every covenant with Satan and witchcraft spirits.

I break and destroy every covenant with witchcraft spirits through the bloodline.

I break and destroy every curse in my life, on the basis of the scriptures that cannot be broken (Galatians 3:13).

By divine authority, I terminate and destroy any witchcraft covenant that has been established in the womb of my mother on my behalf by my parents, consciously or unconsciously.

By divine authority, I terminate and destroy any witchcraft covenant made on my behalf by anyone on the day of my birth dedication, christening, and naming ceremony.

I torment and command every witchcraft deposit in my body to come out in the name of Jesus Christ.

I command every witchcraft food, drink, injection, or arrow in my body to come out by fire in the name of Jesus Christ.

I break and destroy any covenant established with any altar in my mother and father's house (Judges 6:25; Jeremiah 32:18).

I destroy any altar that my name has been taken to by wicked men and women.

I confess and repent of the sin of abortion in my life that has opened the door for the spirit of abortion to abort my blessings.

I break and destroy every covenant with the abortion spirit. I break and destroy every curse and cycle of abortion in my life.

I command every deposit of abortion spirit to come out of me—spirit of setback, failure, non-accomplishment, under-achievement, unfruitfulness, barrenness, frustration, poverty—come out of me in the name of Jesus Christ!

I break every covenant with marine spirits and declare that I am married to Christ Jesus and divorce any personality of the marine kingdom that is married to me.

I refuse to have any properties and deposits of marine spirits. By the blood of the eternal covenant, I flush out all marine deposits out of my life in the name of Jesus Christ.

I expose marine deposits hiding in my body by the truth of God's word, which is light.

I torment and command every marine deposit in my body to manifest and come out in the name of Jesus Christ.

I command the spirit of affliction, oppression, infirmity, setback, death, barrenness, unfruitfulness, excessive bleeding, lust, fornication/sexual immorality, menstrual complications, rebellion, and witchcraft to come out in the name of Jesus Christ.

By divine authority, I command an end to the affliction in my life and I decree and declare that affliction will not rise up for the second time (Nahum 1:9).

I break and destroy any covenant of death in my life in the name of Jesus Christ (Isaiah 28:18).

I command the spirit of untimely death to come out in the name of Jesus Christ.

I command and flush every seed and plant of sickness and disease out of my body in the name of Jesus Christ.

I command the spirits of infirmity, cancer, arthritis, diabetes, heart failure, kidney failure, nerve failure, ulcers, stroke, barrenness, schizophrenia, or memory loss to come out of me in the name of Jesus Christ.

I command any seed and plant of witchcraft in my body to burn to ashes, perish, and come out as liquid and air in the name of Jesus Christ.

I break and terminate the covenant of accidents and command the spirit of accidents to come out in the name of Jesus Christ.

I break and destroy every satanic and witchcraft network against my life, family, and ministry in the name of Jesus Christ.

I command restoration of all stolen goods of mine (Joel 2:25; Job 20:15).

I command a thousand-fold increase upon my life, family, and ministry.

I decree and declare total deliverance in my life, family, and ministry today in the name of Jesus Christ.

I decree and declare an end to the activities of Satan and his demons in my life. Any spirit that has gone out of me cannot re-enter, by the power of the blood of the eternal covenant.

I command the manifestations of the fruits of my total deliverance!

Thank You, Jesus Christ, the captain of my warfare, for my total deliverance.

I decree divine presence, protection, favour, and provision in my life from today onward.